DISCARD

DATE DUE

GAYLORD PRINTED IN U.S.A.

4

5

6

7

8

9

10

11

12

13

14

practical modern CROCHET

practical modern CROCHET

Vibeke Lind

VAN NOSTRAND REINHOLD COMPANY
NEW YORK CINCINNATI TORONTO LONDON MELBOURNE

Van Nostrand Reinhold Company Regional Offices:
New York Cincinnati Chicago Millbrae Dallas
Van Nostrand Reinhold Company International Offices:
London Toronto Melbourne

Copyright © 1973 by Litton Educational Publishing, Inc.
Library of Congress Catalog Card Number: 72-9376
ISBN 0-442-29971-0 (paper); 0-442-29970-2 (hard cover)

All rights reserved. No part of this work covered by the copyright hereon may be reproduced or used in any form or by any means—graphic, electronic, or mechanical, including photocopying, recording, taping, or information storage and retrieval systems—without written permission of the publisher. Manufactured in the United States of America.

Drawings by the author
Photographs by Jens Bull
Designed by Rosa Delia Vasquez

Published by Van Nostrand Reinhold Company
A Division of Litton Educational Publishing, Inc.
450 West 33rd Street, New York, N.Y. 10001
Published simultaneously in Canada by
Van Nostrand Reinhold Company Ltd.
7 9 11 13 15 16 14 12 10 8 6

Contents

INTRODUCTION	14
1. TO BEGIN WITH	15
Materials	
Terminology and Abbreviations	
Basic Techniques	
2. STITCH UNITS AND THEIR VARIATIONS	24
Net Crochet in Chain Stitch	
Slip Stitch	
Single Crochet	
Half-Double Crochet	
Double Crochet	
Triple Crochet and Higher Stitches	
3. PATTERN STITCHES AND ADVANCED TECHNIQUES	36
Stitches Made by Working Around the Post	
Cluster Stitches	
Casting-on in Various Stitches	
Tunisian, or Afghan, Crochet (Tricot)	
4. IDEAS AND PATTERNS	44
Four Crocheted Belts:	
String Belt, Tarred-Twine Belt, Fish-Netting Belt,	
Linen Warp-Thread Belt (Patterns 1—4)	
Crochet with Twine and Wooden Beads:	
Narrow Beaded Band, Wide Beaded Band, Shoulder Bag of	
Tarred Twine (Patterns 5—7)	
Joining-On and Changing Yarn: Rug in Streaks of Color	
Matching Hat and Scarf (Patterns 8—9)	
Poncho Capes:	
Poncho, Child's Poncho, Poncho in Broad Stripes	
(Patterns 10—12)	
Finishing with Edgings, Picots, and Knots	
Crocheted Cords:	
A Rug that turns into a Cape (Pattern 13)	
Crochet in Squares and Circles:	
Square Pot Holder, Round Pot Holder (Patterns 14—15)	
Casting-on in a Ring that can be Drawn Closed:	
Flat Sisal Cushion, Strong Garden Basket of Sisal	
(Patterns 16—17)	
Small Mat and Decorative Cushion in Sisal (Patterns 18—19)	
Irregular Circle Shapes:	
"Knee-Warmer" Rug, Square Cushion, Rectangular Cushion,	
Two Cushions in Spiral Crochet (Patterns 20—24)	
Filling in an Outline in Free Crochet:	
Vest (Waistcoat), Baby's Traveling Bag Lined with	
Lambskin, Large Rug (Patterns 25—27)	
Decorative Banding and Flower Shapes:	
Hat in Patterned Bands, Cushion with Diagonal Stripes,	
Flowered Shawl, Flowered Cap, Summer Cap, Cushion with	
Flower Heads (Patterns 28—33)	
Rosettes and Flower Figures:	
Four Rosette Patterns, Classical Rosette in New Form,	
Bag with Rosette Base, Rosette Cushion (Patterns 34—40)	
Free Forms and Free Use of Color:	
Wall Hanging, Winter Sports Helmet (Patterns 41—42)	
Stuffed Figures in Crochet:	
"China" Hen in Nest (Pattern 43)	
COMPARISON OF SIZES OF CROCHET HOOKS AND NUMBERING SYSTEMS	103
SOURCES OF SUPPLY	104

INTRODUCTION

This book is intended to be a visual introduction to the enchanting world of crochet. It gives detailed instructions on how to work the basic forms of crochet stitches, and explains their relationship to each other. At the same time it shows by example what a variety of articles can be created simply with a crochet hook and yarn.

Crochet is so easy to learn that even small children pick it up quickly, and yet it is astonishing what you can create with just the help of a hooked needle. You can make almost anything: blankets, clothes, useful objects and ornamental pieces. There is no limit to the shapes and color combinations you can achieve in crochet.

All the examples given in this book are simple, but each one exhibits some new variation or application of the common crochet stitches, while pointing out the problems likely to arise for the inexperienced worker. Some of the patterns will appeal to the imaginative worker, who likes to create as she works, and others will appeal to those who just like to have something to do with their hands while thinking about something else. Either way, crochet can be a marvelous relaxation.

It is not difficult to do free crochet, making up the pattern as you go, once you have got the rhythm of crochet work into your fingers. Crochet can absorb you so much that you cease to be aware of anything else as long as you are doing it. You can work with a crochet hook as freely as an artist works with his brush or you can make simple, regular rows in a single color. The beauty of the finished work lies in the quality of the yarn and the care taken in the stitching.

1.
TO BEGIN WITH

MATERIALS

HOOKS

Only one sort of tool is needed for crochet work: a crochet hook. They are available in a great many sizes, from the finest steel hooks used for making lace, to the coarsest aluminum or plastic hooks used for bulky yarns.

The system for numbering these hooks varies with the material used to make the hook—steel, aluminum, wood, and plastic—and with the country of manufacture. In this book the new international numbering based on the metric system is used because it is the clearest. If the width of a crochet hook (hook end) is 6mm, the hook is called a number 6. A chart in the back of the book shows the relation between crochet hooks and numbering systems in the United States, United Kingdom, and in the International Numbering system. A number 7, for example, would be an J or a 10 in the U.S. and a 2 in the U.K.

It does not cost very much to have a good selection of crochet hooks on hand. As there are half sizes available, a good selection from the small 3mm hooks to the largest 9mm hooks would include about 10 to 12 different sizes in all.

You can keep your crochet hooks out in a small jar on your work table, as shown in the drawing. This is both attractive and practical. If you want to try out some new kind of yarn, it is nice to be able to pick the right size hook in the same way a painter chooses his brush.

If you do a lot of crochet, it is very important to use a crochet hook that feels comfortable in your hand. It must be neither too light nor too heavy in relation to the yarn you are using. If it is wrong for the yarn, it will cause you fatigue. However, the right choice is a very individual matter, depending on how tightly you crochet. As you get more experience you will loosen up. It is important to sit in a relaxed position while you are working so that your muscles won't tighten up and make the tension on the stitches too tight.

A variety of crochet hooks should be in easy reach

YARNS

There are a wide variety of suitable yarns to choose from. All knitting yarns can be used for crochet, but you can also use packing twine—from ordinary cord to thick sisal. Out-of-the-ordinary yarns can be found in marine supply stores and other suppliers of materials for different handcrafts.

Any piece of work will look better if the yarn is appropriate for the purpose to which the article will be put. Strong, coarse materials will look best in a simple country setting, whereas finer threads and more sophisticated color effects will be more suitable in a town or city.

In most of the patterns in this book natural yarns have been used—pure wool weaving yarn or rug wool. In addition to wearing well they have the great advantage that their color range is constant over the years. In knitting wool, the colors manufactured are subject to the dictates of fashion. In weaving yarns there is a wide choice of colors and far more shade variations available.

The photograph shows most of the yarns used in the models for the patterns. If the specific yarn or thread is not available, substitutes can always be used. A list of suppliers is given at the back of the book.

Yarn 1 is a thin 2-ply wool used in Pattern 13. It is a weaving wool, approximately the size of crewel embroidery yarn or fingering yarn.

Yarn 2 is a 2-ply weaving wool used in the majority of patterns for small articles: Patterns 8, 9, 10, 11, 12, 20, 21, 22, 25, 27, 30, and 31. This medium-sized 2-ply yarn is about the size of 3-ply persian wool used in tapestry. An ordinary thin knitting worsted can be substituted, but remember that it is harder to crochet with a 4-ply yarn than with a 3- or 2-ply yarn.

Yarn 3 is a rya wool. It is a rough textured 2-ply yarn for rugs, which can be found in imports from European countries. A 2- or 3-ply medium-sized sport yarn can be substituted. It is used in Patterns 23, 24, 28, 29, and 33.

Yarn 4 is a 3-ply rug wool or thick rya wool used in Patterns 26 and 42. Rug wool or bulky sport yarn is a good substitute.

Yarn 5 is a thin natural (handspun) wool used in Patterns 26 and 43. Specialty wool suppliers will probably carry such yarn. There are some synthetics on the market which are also very loosely spun, and can be used as an experiment.

Yarn 6 is a thicker natural wool, also used in Patterns 26 and 43.

Yarn 7 is Mayflower cotton Number 8. Any ordinary mercerized crochet cotton can substitute. It is used in Patterns 14 and 15. The pearlized crochet cotton (not shown) is used in Patterns 34, 35, 36, 37.

Yarn 8 is fish-netting used in Pattern 3. The real thing will have to be purchased in a marine supply store, but a nonshiny highly mercerized cotton is a good substitute.

Yarn 9 is coarse linen yarn used in Patterns 32, 40, and 41. A specialty store might carry this, as it is sometimes used in weaving. Carpet warp and upholsterer's cord (not shown) can substitute. The upholsterer's cord is used in Pattern 1.

Yarn 10 is thin tarred twine used in Patterns 5 and 6. It can be obtained in marine supply stores. Butcher's twine will do as a substitute, but if you want the smooth surface given by the tarring, you will have to experiment with some of the synthetic twines and cords.

Yarn 11 is a linen warp thread used in Patterns 4, 38, 39, and 40. A weaving supply store may have this, or you can substitute carpet warp or thin cord.

Yarn 12 is coarse tarred twine used in Patterns 2 and 7, and can be obtained in marine supply stores. Upholsterer's cord does not have the smooth surface, but it is very heavy and comes in a dark brown color. For experimentation, a thin macramé cord of a dark color might be used.

Yarn 13 is sisal cord used in Patterns 16 and 19. Sisal is used to make many types of packing and wrapping cord, and is sold in most variety stores.

Yarn 14 is thick sisal cord used in Patterns 17 and 18. It, too, can be found in most variety stores.

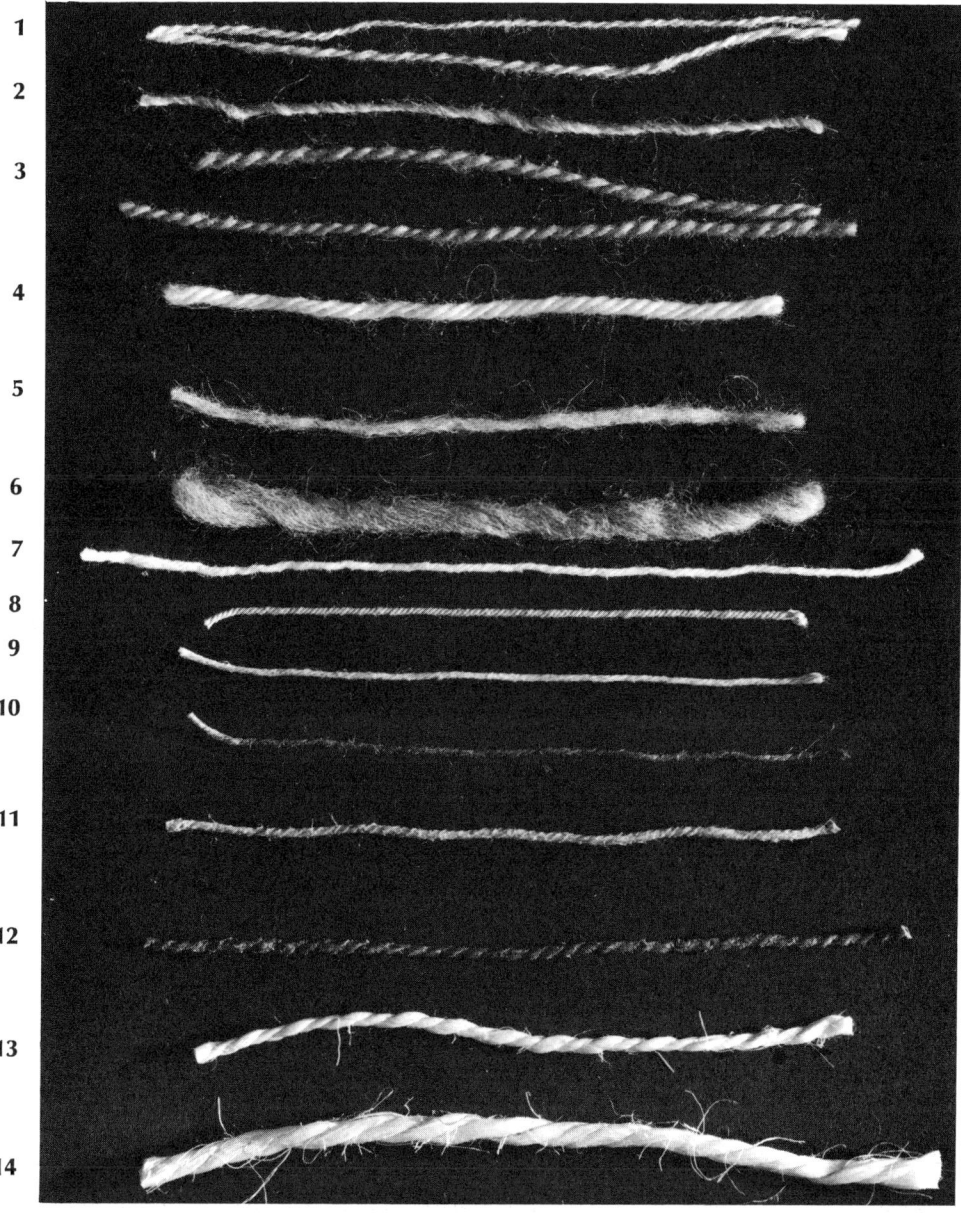

Yarns used in the models in this book. *From the top:* thin 2-ply wool, rya wool, 2-ply weaving wool, 3-ply rug wool, thin natural wool, thicker natural wool, Mayflower cotton, fish-netting, coarse linen yarn, thin tarred twine, linen warp thread, coarse tarred twine, sisal cord, thick sisal cord

YARNS AND STITCHES PROVIDE VARIETY

Just how wide a range of finished effects is produced by all the different yarns and stitches will be seen from the different examples of crochet illustrated here.

Chain stitch worked in fine mohair appears like small rings because of the elasticity of the yarn. The open pattern combined with the fineness and lightness of the yarn is particularly suitable for scarves and small shawls.

Slip stitch and single crochet worked in the round make a firm combination suitable for belts and bags that will have heavy wear. The insertion of the hook was made in the back loop of the stitch, and the yarn is colored fish netting.

A pattern consisting of single crochet and chain stitch combined gives an attractive texture suitable for large articles of clothing or, in thick woolen yarn, for throws. The single crochet was worked under the chain stitches of the preceding row.

A narrow braid or ribbon can be used for crochet in small articles such as hats. It is considerably more expensive than yarn. The model is worked in single crochet in which the rows are alternated between insertion in the front loop and insertion in the back loop of the stitch in the previous row. The simple style allows the material to show to advantage.

A reversed shell pattern worked in double crochet in thin woolen yarn would be attractive for a small blanket or a small shawl to wrap around a baby.

Double crochet stitches in tunisian crochet with thick natural yarn is particularly suitable for baby carriage covers. The hand-spinning produces a very fuzzy texture in the yarn, and the stitch (sometimes called afghan crochet or tricot) is firm enough to make a very warm material.

Chain stitch worked in a fine mohair

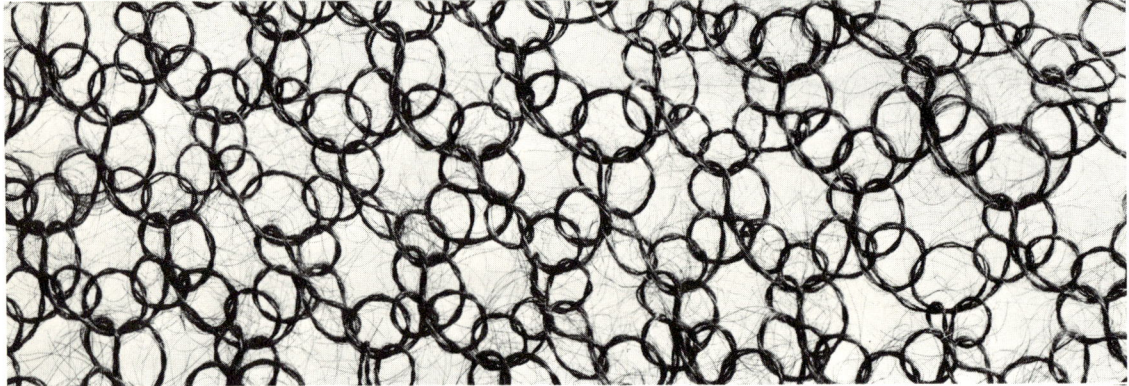

Slip stitch and single crochet in fish-netting. The double rows of stitches lying flat are the slip stitches

Single crochet and chain stitches combined give an attractive texture

Single crochet worked in a fine braided cord. The insertion of the hook was alternated from the front to the back loop of the stitches

Reversed shell pattern in double crochet

Tunisian, or afghan, crochet worked in handspun wool in double crochet

TERMINOLOGY AND ABBREVIATIONS

All crochet stitches are based on a single unit. The hook is inserted into a stitch or group of stitches, and a new loop is pulled through the loop already on the hook. Before the hook is pushed through the stitch it may be wrapped with yarn, and a new loop pulled through more than a single time. The height of the stitch increases with the number of wraps.

The drawing shows a row of crochet stitches consisting of a slip stitch, a single crochet, a half-double crochet, a double crochet, a triple crochet, and a double-triple crochet. The difference between the heights can be seen clearly, and by making use of this difference you can vary the outline of the edge of a piece of crochet. You might want to do this when working from a paper pattern or following some other irregular outline.

Height of stitches, *from right to left:* slip stitch, single crochet, half-double crochet, double crochet, triple crochet, and double-triple crochet

The stitches are not always called by the same names in different countries. Even if you have been taught a different name for a stitch than the one used here, you can easily figure out what it is by looking at the picture and referring to the following list.

Slip Stitch is sometimes called a Single Crochet
(no wrap, draw through 2 loops on hook at once)

Single Crochet   Double Crochet
(no wrap, draw through 1 and then 2 loops)

Half-double Crochet   Half-treble Crochet
(1 wrap, draw through 1 and then 3 loops)

Double Crochet   Treble Crochet
(1 wrap, draw through 1, then 2, then 2 loops)

Triple Crochet   Double-treble Crochet
(2 wraps, draw through 1, then 2, then 2, then 2 loops)

Double-triple Crochet   Triple-treble Crochet
(3 wraps, draw through 1 loop, then 2 at once 4 times)

Triple-triple Crochet   Quadruple-treble Crochet
(4 wraps, draw through 1 loop, then 2 at once 5 times)

ABBREVIATIONS

Abbreviations are often used in printed crochet patterns. In order to facilitate reading, only a few abbreviations are used in this book, but here is a list of those in general use.

r	row
rnd	round
st	stitch
sts	stitches
ch	chain stitch
ss	slip stitch
sc	single crochet
h dc	half-double crochet
dc	double crochet
tr	triple crochet
dbl tr	double-triple crochet
tr tr	triple-triple crochet
over or yarn over	wrap hook by bringing yarn forward over it (this is sometimes abbreviated y.o.)
2 tog	make two stitches together, equaling one
dec	decrease
inc	increase
rep	repeat
*	repeat instruction from * to the next *
3 (5 dc, 2 tog)	make five double crochet, then work the next two together, and repeat the sequence two more times
2 x 3 sc in next st	make three single crochets in each stitch for three stitches along the chain or previous row

BASIC TECHNIQUES

In crochet, as in knitting, one continuous thread is looped in various ways to form the entire fabric. In practice, the yarn may be changed when one skein runs out or a color change is necessary. In principle, however, the piece is made from a single thread. Every crochet stitch ends in a loop which remains on the crochet hook, after which the next stitch may be formed. This kind of crochet is by far the commonest, and is known as single-loop crochet or ordinary crochet.

Another method, possibly the older, consists of casting-on a number of stitches, one after the other, so that all the loops remain on the crochet hook. A special hook as long as a knitting needle is used for this. After the casting-on row, or forward row, each loop is worked off the hook one by one, until only one loop remains. This kind of crochet comes from Africa. It is an elementary form of knitting and is known as multi-stitch crochet, tunisian crochet, afghan crochet, or tricot.

Ordinary crochet consists of different basic stitches, of which the chain stitch is the simplest and is used as the foundation row in most cases. The slip stitch and the single crochet are developed from the chain stitch. The stitch that is formed by wrapping the hook, the double crochet, can be varied in a number of ways. The half-double, the triple, and the wound and cluster stitches are developed from it.

Each of the stitches (except the chain) can be varied according to the way in which the hook is passed through the stitch which forms its base. In addition, any number of patterns may be formed by different combinations of the different stitches. In tunisian crochet, different stitches can be produced by varying the way in which the hook is inserted in the forward row and also the way the loops are worked off in the return row.

POSITION OF THE HANDS
Hold the hook in your right hand in the same way you would hold a pen, and put it through the loop, holding the work between thumb and middle finger of the left hand. Lay the yarn over the first finger. You will then be able to use the first finger, moving it up and down, to regulate the supply of yarn. In working with smooth-surfaced yarns it may be a help to wind the yarn around the little finger before passing it over the first finger. This will give you better control of the tension.

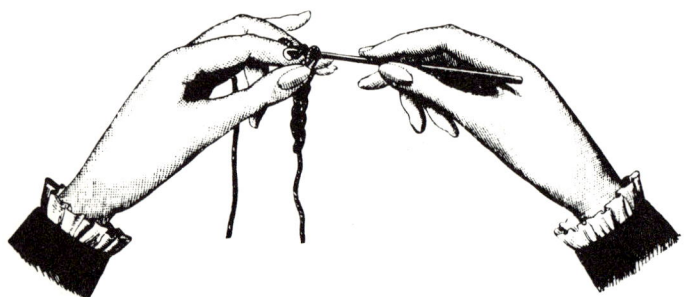

Traditional position of the hands in crochet

CASTING-ON IN CHAIN STITCH
The first row or round of a piece must be cast on before the second row can be built upon it, as described above. Chain stitch is generally used for casting-on, the other stitches being worked into these. A certain number of chain stitches are also used at the end of each row, to bring the work into position for the next row. Take the yarn as shown in the drawing. Hold it firmly at the point where the yarn crosses between the thumb and middle finger of the left hand, and let it lie over the first finger. Pass the hook through the loop, under the yarn lying over the first finger, and draw the yarn through the loop.

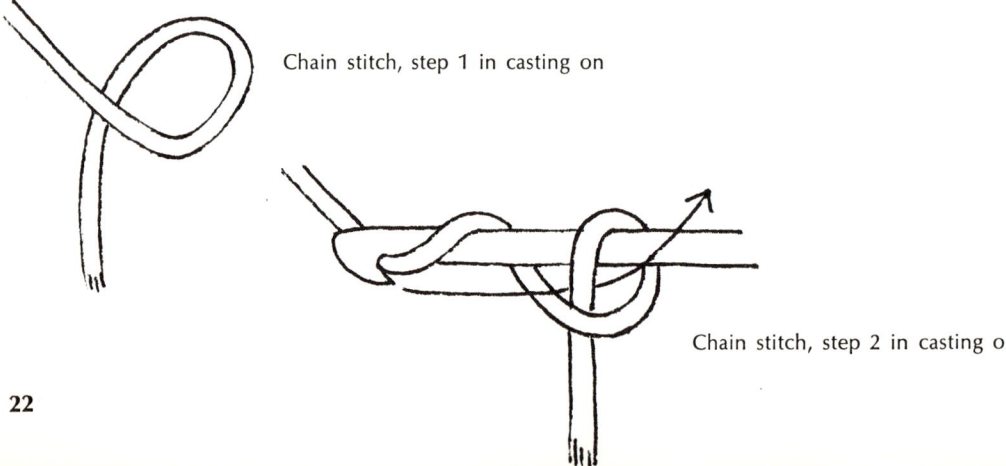

Chain stitch, step 1 in casting on

Chain stitch, step 2 in casting on

You now have a loop on the hook, which is then passed over the yarn again—catch the yarn in the hook and draw it back through the loop, thereby forming a new loop. Continue in this way until you have the required number of chain stitches on the foundation row.

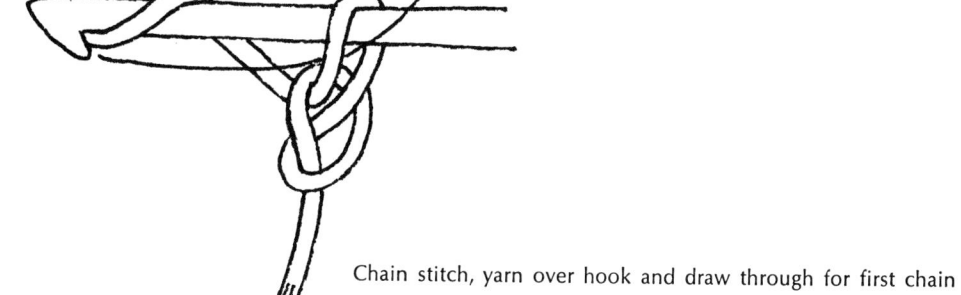

Chain stitch, yarn over hook and draw through for first chain

Chain stitch, continue the cast-on row until you have the required length for the foundation

The drawing shows the casting-on, or foundation, row, with the first stitch about to be worked into the last chain stitch but one of the casting-on row. This is the method used for turning the piece when the second row is started.

Chain stitch, starting the 2nd row

2.
STITCH UNITS & THEIR VARIATIONS

NET CROCHET IN CHAIN STITCH

Chain stitch can be used to form a pattern in itself. Here is a pattern in which a number of short lengths of chain stitches have been worked so as to form a network. This is suitable for use with light, soft yarns in articles such as scarves and shawls. It can be used with coarse yarns to make such things as nets for ball games or open shopping bags.

Cast-on row: a number of ch sts divisible by 4, then work 5 more ch for turning.

2nd row: 1 sc into the 3rd st from the end of the cast-on row, *5 ch, skip 2 ch in the cast-on row, 1 sc.*

Succeeding rows: 5 ch to turn, then *1 sc into the middle of the 5 ch in the preceding row, 5 ch.*

Net, or filet, crochet in chain stitch and single crochet

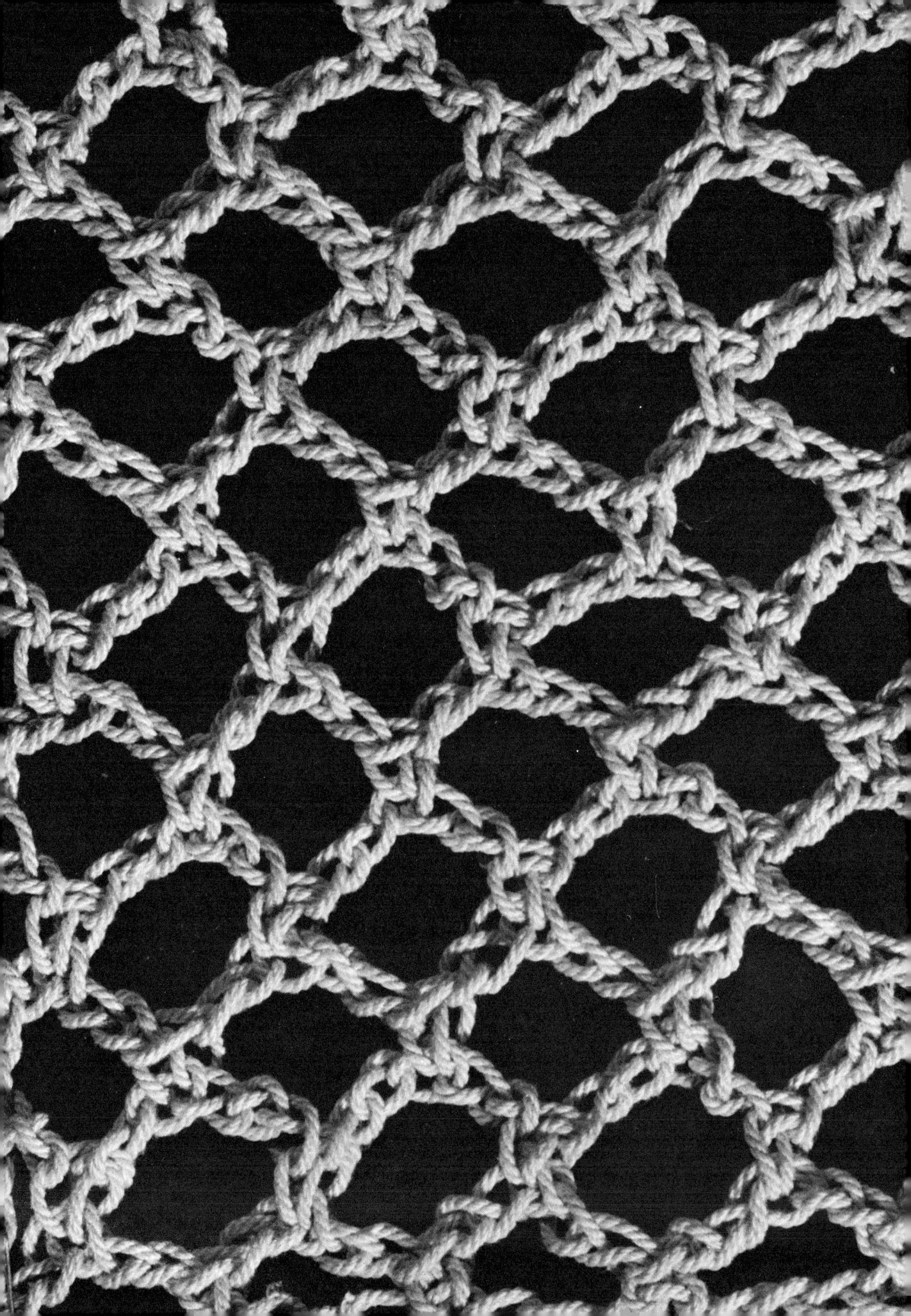

SLIP STITCH

To begin a slip stitch, insert the hook into the last stitch but one of the row of chain stitches. Bring the hook under the yarn lying across the first finger, and draw the yarn back through the stitch and at the same time through the loop on the hook.

As will be seen from the drawing, slip stitch (and every stitch in crochet) leaves a loop on the hook. When the next stitch is worked, this loop is closed. The edge of a row of crochet will thus be formed of a row of closed loops, and these loops will be the basis of the next row.

A slip stitch is very low. It lies almost directly on top of the row it is worked into, with almost no height. Consequently, it makes very firm fabric, and is quite hard to do over a large surface.

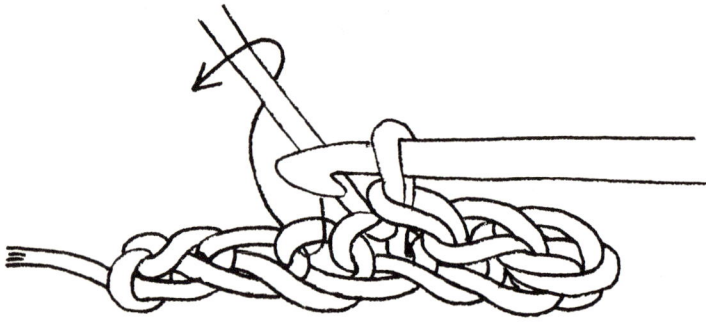

Slip stitch, step 1

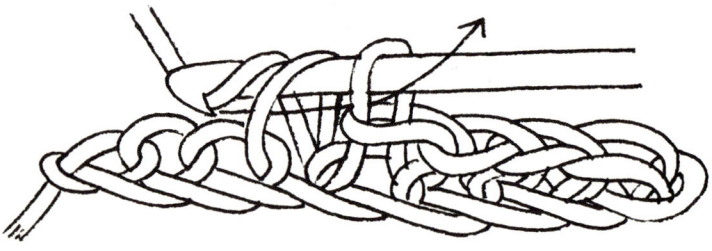

Slip stitch, step 2

The lowness also gives the stitch its usefulness as a decoration. A simple row of slip stitch, worked a little way in from the edge will look like a row of chain-stitch embroidery. At the edge it is particularly suitable for a firm, inelastic border. Slip stitches are used to close a ring of chain stitches or a round of any stitch in crochet as invisibly as possible. They can also be used, if you wish to avoid breaking the yarn, when ending or changing colors, to carry the yarn along "invisibly" a little way, in order to start working a few stitches farther along.

To make a slip stitch (or any stitch in crochet) you can either insert the hook under both the front and the back threads of the loop, or only under the front loop, or only under the back loop. The surface of the fabric will look quite different in each of these cases. Used as a pattern stitch, the low loops give a closely woven effect. Slip stitch must always be worked from the same side. It will be seen from the photograph how the horizontal rows will result if you work into the back loop (marked black on the drawing), and the vertical pattern that is formed if you work into the front loop (shaded on the drawing).

Slip stitch can be used to make an attractive cord for ties, little bows, and so forth. Make the cast-on row to the required length and then work either one or two rows of slip stitch. Work always from the same side, instead of working to and fro by reversing the fabric to turn. Work always into the back loop, which is shown in black in the drawing. If you would like to vary the patterns, work into the front loop or alternate in some way.

Slip stitch gives a low-lying row of closely woven loops

Slip stitch can be worked into the back (black) loop or the front (hatched) loop

Slip stitch results in a pattern of horizontal rows if worked in the back loop and vertical rows if worked in the front loop

SINGLE CROCHET

Single crochet is probably the most commonly used stitch, and gives a firm and solid character to the work. It stands a little higher than a slip stitch, about the height of 1 chain stitch.

Insert the hook into a stitch, wrap the yarn around the hook and draw it through the stitch, wrap the yarn over the hook again, and draw the yarn (the new loop) through both loops on the hook.

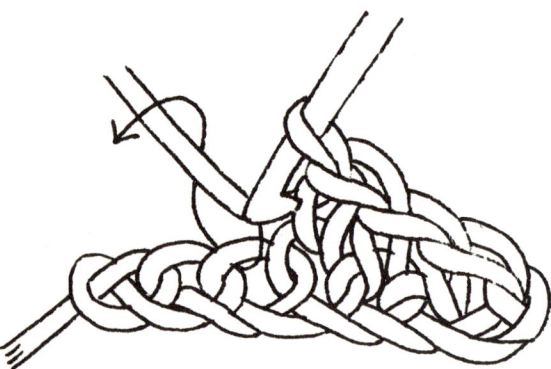

Single crochet, step 1

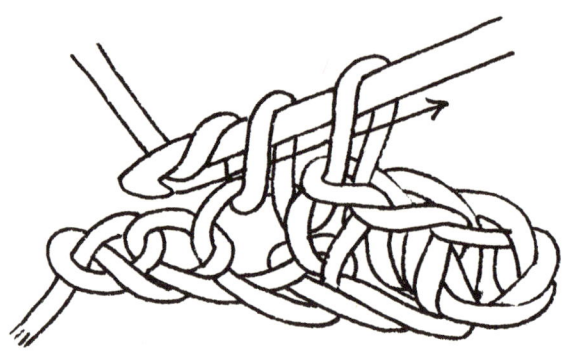

Single crochet, step 2

Rose stitch is the name given to the commonest form of single crochet, which is worked to and fro in rows. The hook is passed under both loops of the stitch in the preceding row, which gives firmness and strength to the work.

Single crochet can be varied in a number of ways. Like slip stitch, the hook can be inserted under both the loops of the stitch, (non-ribbed single crochet) or under only the back (ribbed single crochet). The way in which the yarn is passed around the hook can also be varied, and will vary the appearance of the work. The fabric will also look different if you crochet to and fro in rows or in rounds. To make good edges when working in rows, you should be careful to put the yarn in front of the work each time you turn.

The following examples and descriptions are of the most characteristic forms of single crochet. Every worker will eventually find her own favorites among the many variations.

Rows of single crochet are sometimes called rose stitch

CROSSED SINGLE CROCHET
Unlike ordinary crochet, in which the hook is passed under the yarn ("yarn over hook"), here the hook is passed over the yarn producing a crossed appearance.

Crossed single crochet

SINGLE CROCHET WORKED IN THE ROUND, OR ALWAYS FROM THE SAME SIDE
Working in the round is done when you want a circular basis for the article you are making, such as a hat. Working in a circle means that you are always working from the same side of the piece. Even though the hook is passed under both loops of the stitch as in rose stitch, the result is quite different.

Single crochet worked always from the same side (or in the round) looks different from rose stitch that is worked to and fro

RIBBED SINGLE CROCHET
While working to and fro in rows, pass the hook only through the back loop of the stitch in the preceding row. This throws the body of the loop forward and gives a strong relief effect. Each new row lies almost at right angles to the row before.

Ribbed single crochet, worked to and fro

HALF-DOUBLE CROCHET

Wrap the yarn around the hook, and insert the hook in the loop of a stitch in the preceding row. Wrap the yarn over again, and draw it back through the loop of the stitch. Make another over, and draw the yarn through all three loops on the hook.

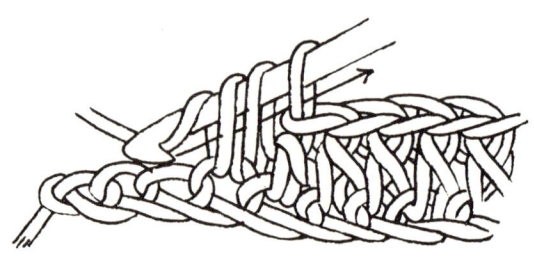

Half-double crochet, drawing through yarn

VARIATIONS OF HALF-DOUBLE CROCHET
If the hook is inserted under a loop at the back of the stitch in the preceding row, the edge loops will lie at the front of the work.

The drawing shows which loop to take at the back of the work. Crochet all the time from the same side to obtain this effect. The photograph shows the finished work.

Half-double crochet, showing loop to pick up for this effect

This variation of half-double crochet is always worked from the same side

An attractive effect can be produced by working to and fro, always into the front loop.

Half-double crochet, worked to and fro in front loop

The striped effect will not be quite so pronounced if you work to and fro, under both loops.

Half-double crochet, worked to and fro under both loops

JOINED HALF-DOUBLE CROCHET (DOUBLE HALF-TREBLES)
A variation of the half-double stitch that gives a stronger fabric is made by crocheting twice into each stitch in the previous row, in the following way.

Wrap the yarn over the hook, and insert it into the loop of the first stitch, make an over, and draw the yarn through. Put the hook into the second stitch. Make an over and draw the yarn through, make an over, and draw the yarn through all 4 loops on the hook at once. Work the next stitch in the same way, now putting the hook the first time into the stitch that was second before. Joined half-doubles are very suitable for edgings on such articles as hats.

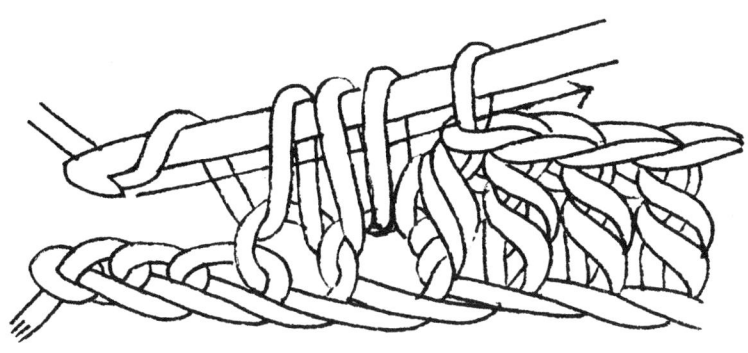

Joined half-double crochet, drawing through yarn

DOUBLE CROCHET

Wrap the yarn around the hook. Put the hook into the loop of the stitch in the previous row. Make an over, draw the hook back through the loop of the stitch. Make another over, and draw the yarn through the first 2 loops. Make an over, and draw the yarn through the 2 remaining loops.

This stitch is 1 step higher than a half-double crochet, about the height of 2-3 chains. Consequently, at the beginning of each new row, work a number of chain stitches corresponding to the height of the succeeding stitches. That is to say, for double crochet work 3 chain stitches to turn.

When it is worked under both loops of the stitch, there is not much difference between double crochet worked to and fro and that worked in the round. The example shown is worked backwards and forwards (to and fro).

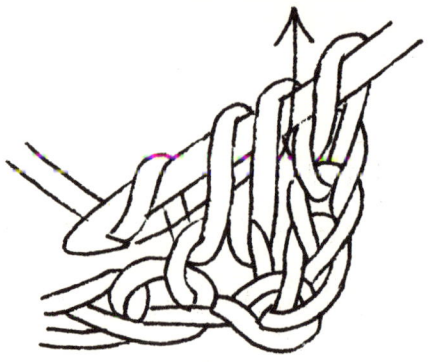

Double crochet, step 1

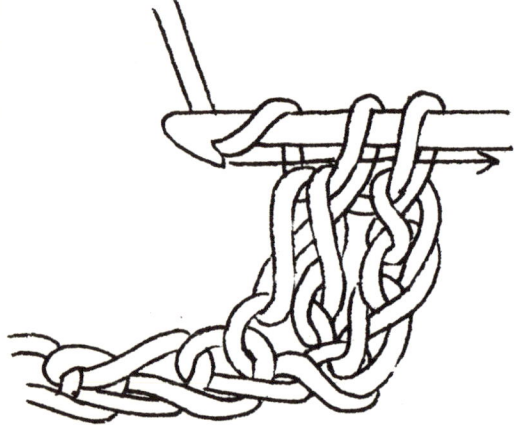

Double crochet, step 2

A double crochet is the height of 3 chain stitches approximately

Double crochet, worked to and fro under both loops

DOUBLE CROCHET UNDER BACK LOOP

Double crochet can be worked under the back loop or the front loop. Here we see double crochet worked under the back loop, to and fro. This throws the front loop strongly forward. On the reverse row the loop will be thrown to the back of the fabric, and together the rows will produce a striped effect across the surface of the work.

Double crochet, worked under the back loop

WORKING BETWEEN THE STITCHES

As a result of the first pass of the yarn over the hook there is always a little loop running between the finished stitches, which is marked black in the drawing. This offers the possibility for more variations than can be made with single crochet. You can insert the hook under both loops, under the front loop, under the back loop, or under the loop that runs between the stitches.

A hook can be inserted under the black thread or between the thread and the stitch, which is the usual form of crochet

The last alternative is called working between the stitches, or working into the space. The effect is to make the individual stitches stand out more.

When worked under this thread, the technique is called "working between the stitches" or "working into the space"

In the usual forms of crochet, the stitch is worked down only into the loops of the stitch below, making the stitches stand almost vertically above one another.

When worked between the thread and the loops of the stitch, which is the usual form of crochet, the individual stitches stand almost vertically above one another

WORKING AROUND THE POST
The height of the double crochet stitch forms a stem, or post. This allows you to insert the hook from the side rather than from the top of the stitch. The insertion can be made from the front, around behind the post, and out the front again—this is called working from front to back—or it can be made from behind, around the front, and out the back again. This is called working from back to front.

When working from the front, the edge loops are hidden at the back of the work. When working from the back, the edge loops form a line running across the work, and the row you are working on will lie horizontally on top of the preceding row. This may be turned to account where strongly marked edgings are required.

Working from front to back, around the post

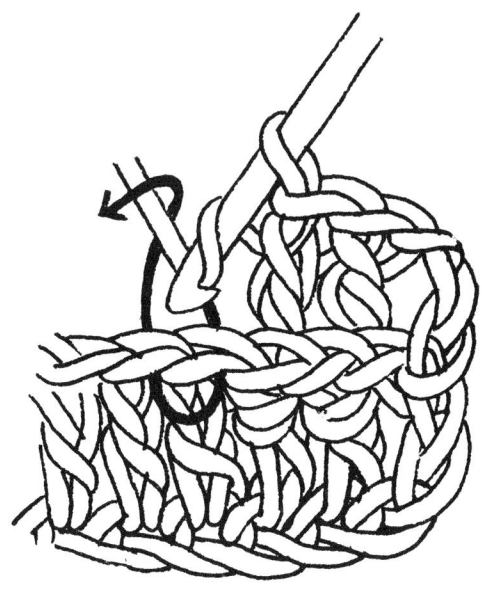
Working from back to front, around the post

TRIPLE CROCHET AND HIGHER STITCHES

To work triples, start with 4-5 chain stitches. Pass the yarn twice over the hook, and put it into the loop of the stitch. Make an over, and draw the loop back onto the hook. Make an over and draw the yarn through 2 loops. Make an over again, and again draw the yarn through 2 loops. Make an over and draw the yarn through the last 2 loops on the hook.

To make a double-triple crochet, pass the yarn 3 times around the hook and work off 2 loops at a time. To make a triple-triple crochet, pass the yarn 4 times around the hook, and work off 2 loops at a time. See the drawing on page 20, illustrating the height of different stitches.

All of the variations that have been described for double crochet can be worked in higher stitches as well.

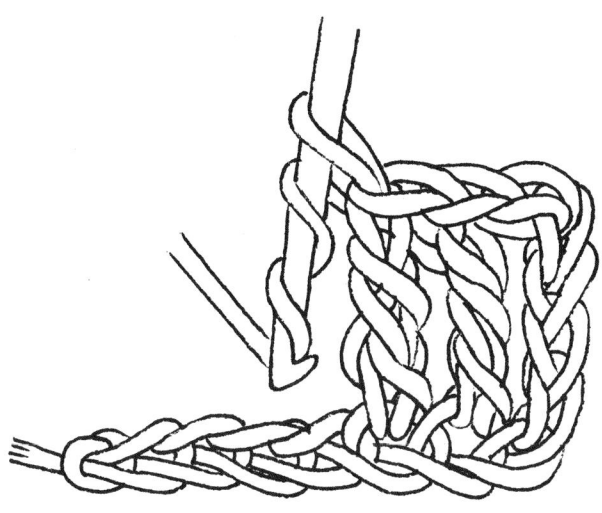
Triple crochet, wrapping the hook

3.

PATTERN STITCHES & ADVANCED TECHNIQUES

STITCHES MADE BY WORKING AROUND THE POST

CABLE STITCH
Work a row of ordinary double crochet. Work 2 chain stitches to turn, equaling the height of a double crochet. Make an over, insert the hook from the front, between the first and second double of the previous row, and out again between the second and third double. Make an over, and work a double in the ordinary way. This second row forms the front of the pattern.

3rd row: 2 ch to turn, work another row of dc, but this time put the hook in from behind in front of the stitch, and out at the back of the piece (working from back to front).

Cable stitch can also be worked with triple or double-triple crochet.

Cable stitch is double crochet worked around the post

BASKET-WEAVE PATTERN
In this pattern, the two kinds of insertion around the post alternate, 3 stitches being worked from the back and 3 from the front in sequence. Every third row the pattern is reversed, which gives a woven effect.

The basket-weave pattern results from alternating the insertions for the cable stitch, from the front and from the back

WOUND-SHELL STITCH

Yet another variation of the double stitch, the so-called wound-shell stitch, can be made by using the post of the double crochet as a base, and working around and around it. This produces a thick knot or twisted stitch which can be used as an ornament.

The wound-shell stitch uses the post of the double crochet as a base

Work an ordinary double crochet, make an over, and draw a loop onto the hook by working around the double crochet you have just made. Repeat this another 4-5 times. After the last over, draw the yarn through all the loops on the hook at once. Make another over, and draw the yarn through the last loop on the hook. There is a similar stitch, called a bullion-bar stitch, that uses this winding principle without working around the post. Instead, multiple insertions are made into a chain stitch.

Here is a pattern, with double crochets worked under both loops, that uses the wound-shell stitch.

1st row: dc

2nd row: alternately 1 dc and 1 wound-shell stitch made with 4 loops on the post of the dc

Wound-shell stitch, wrapping the double crochet

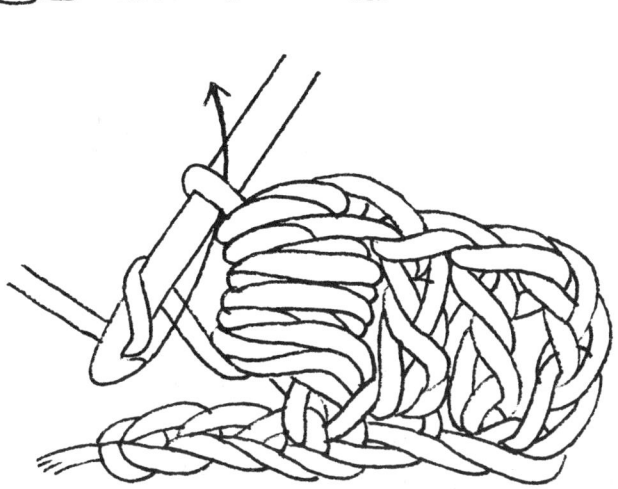

Wound-shell stitch, drawing the wrapped stitch closed

Wound-shell stitch, closed

CLUSTER STITCHES

By working several doubles into the same loop, a cluster of stitches is obtained, which can either be closed over as a group, so that the stitches lie in a clump, or each be closed separately. In the latter case they will lie open like a fan or shell.

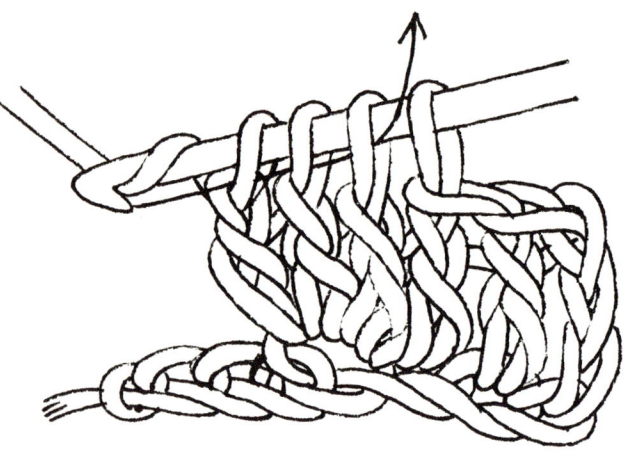

A cluster stitch is basically several stitches worked into the same loop or stitch in the preceding row

CLOSED CLUSTER, OR PINEAPPLE STITCH

After working the first row in double crochet, the pineapple stitch is worked as follows. Make an over, and put the hook into the loop of a stitch in the previous row. Make an over, and draw a loop up onto the hook, over again, and draw the yarn through the first 2 loops, over and draw the yarn through the loop on the hook. Repeat this 4 times. Then wrap the yarn over the hook and draw a loop through the 5 loops already on the hook. Work 1 chain to finish.

Here is a pineapple stitch pattern particularly suitable for long shawls, soft blankets, or throws made with light yarns.

1st row: dc

2nd row: pineapple st, 1 ch, skip one st, and repeat the sequence

Succeeding rows: work a pineapple st in the space between the pineapple sts in the preceding row

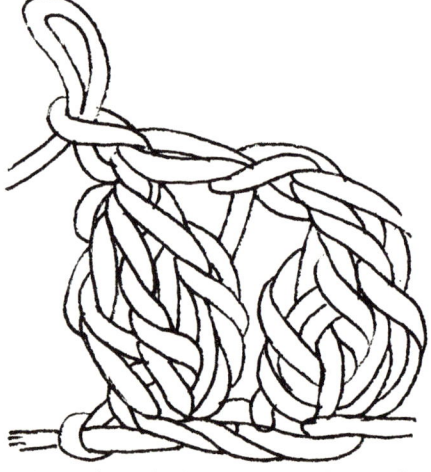

A pineapple stitch made from clusters of 3 stitches

Pineapple stitch is a familiar variation of the basic cluster stitch

OPEN CLUSTER, OR SHELL STITCH

Cast on a number of stitches divisible by 5, and work a group of 7 double crochets in the 3rd chain stitch. Skip over 4 stitches, work another cluster in the 5th, and so on.

So that the cluster stitches can be seen more clearly, work the pattern in two colors, as shown in the photograph. Begin the new color in the 2nd row. Work the 1st cluster in the space between 2 clusters in the preceding row. Work a single crochet in the center of the next cluster, then a cluster in the next space between 2 clusters in the preceding row.

In both open and closed cluster stitches, or decorative stitches as they are sometimes called, the cluster may take up more space along the row than the underlying stitches. In this case, skip over the number of ground stitches that they take up. To get to the middle of a new stitch, a corresponding number of chain stitches must be worked. In working over a large surface, take care that the number of ground stitches in the row following a decorative row corresponds to the original number of ground stitches.

A shell-stitch pattern in 2 colors

Double crochet stitches worked into a shell stitch

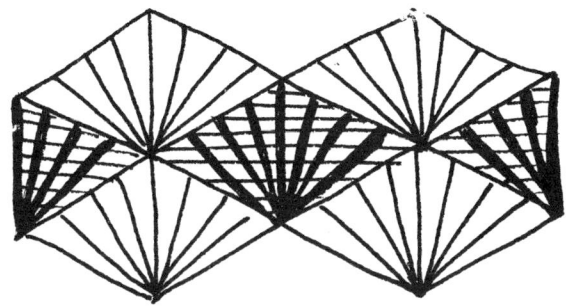

Shell-stitch pattern in 2 colors with 7 stitches in each cluster

CASTING-ON IN VARIOUS STITCHES

To get a more even line of cast-on stitches than can be achieved with chain stitch, you can cast on in single crochet. This is particularly suitable where a long row is required.

If you want a higher and more distinct edge, you can cast on in doubles or in triples.

DOUBLE CHAIN, OR CHAIN OF SINGLE CROCHET

Work 2 chain stitches. Put the hook into the first chain stitch, make an over and draw a loop onto the hook. Make another over and draw the yarn through the 2 loops on the hook.

In the next stitch and each of the succeeding stitches put the hook down into the left-hand loop, as shown in the drawing, and work a single crochet as before.

After working the desired length, work 2 chain to turn, if you are going to work single crochet into the cast-on stitches.

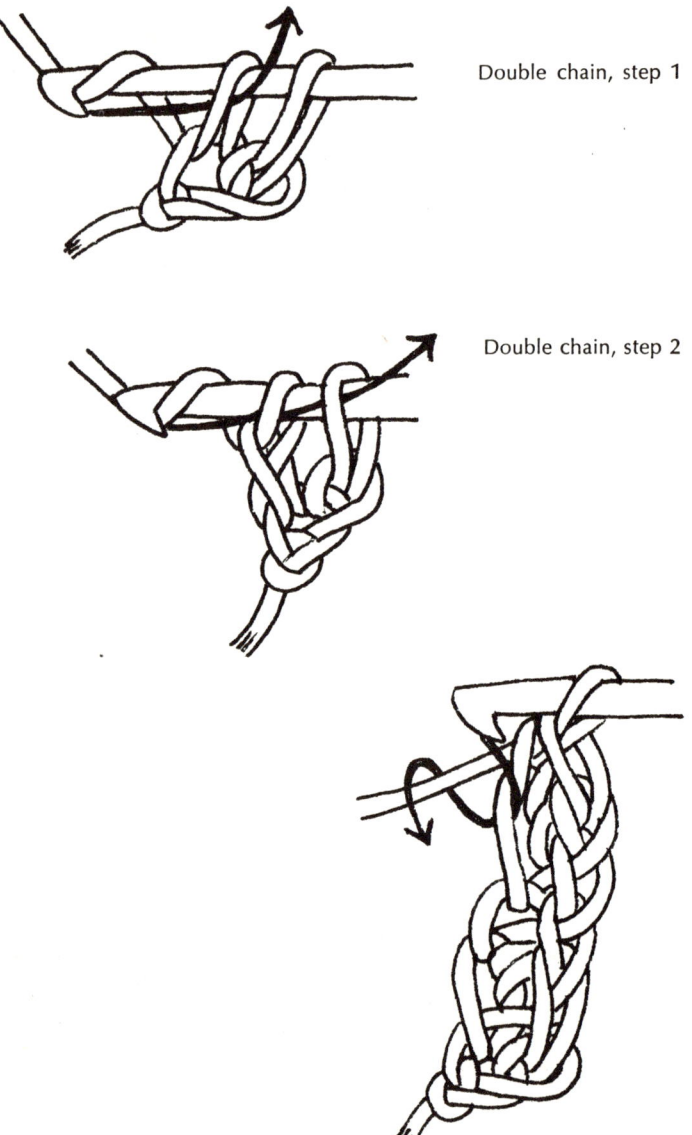

Double chain, step 1

Double chain, step 2

Double chain, step 3, putting the hook into the left-hand loop

Double chain, step 4, working a single crochet

TRIPLE CHAIN, OR CHAIN OF DOUBLE CROCHET

To cast on in double crochet work 3 chain stitches, then work a double crochet into the first chain stitch. In all the succeeding stitches put the hook down into the loop on the extreme left, as shown in the drawing.

To cast on in triples (a double-triple chain) work 4 chain stitches, then work in triples in the same way as for doubles.

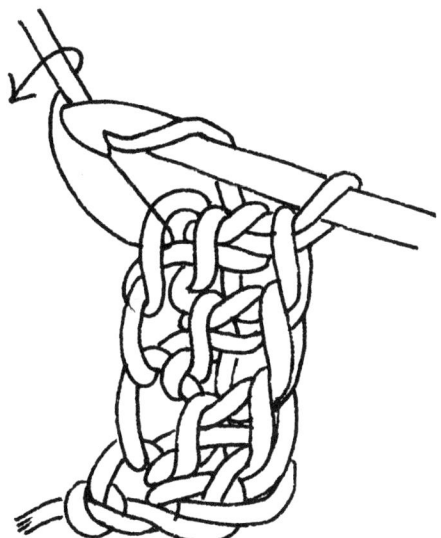

Triple chain, putting the hook into the extreme left-hand loop

Triple chain, working a double crochet

TUNISIAN, OR AFGHAN, CROCHET (TRICOT)

Tunisian crochet is worked in 2 stages, without turning the work. There is a forward, or casting-on row, and a return row. The crochet hook must be long enough to keep all the stitches required for the width of the work on the hook at the same time. Special hooks are made for this purpose.

It may be convenient to make small articles such as belts or handles for bags in tunisian crochet. Larger articles cannot be made with this stitch, without piecing, because their width is too great.

As with ordinary crochet, different effects can be achieved by varying the way in which the hook is inserted in the stitches. Only two forms of tunisian crochet are described here, but once you have mastered the principle, it is not difficult to invent fresh variations for yourself.

Ordinary tunisian, or afghan, crochet gives a closely woven, firm fabric

ORDINARY TUNISIAN CROCHET

Work a row of chain stitches of the desired width. In the 1st row, work 1 chain stitch to turn, then insert the hook in the 1st stitch of the cast-on row and draw a loop onto the hook. Repeat this in each of the following stitches in the row.

Tunisian crochet, forward row completed

On the return row, work the 1st stitch as a closed chain stitch in order to keep the edge even. Then work off the rest of the stitches 2 at a time as follows. Make an over and draw through 2 loops, then repeat this until there is only 1 loop remaining on the hook.

In the 2nd forward row, put the hook through the vertical loops in the preceding row, as shown in the drawing. When the work is long enough, work the last row in slip stitch.

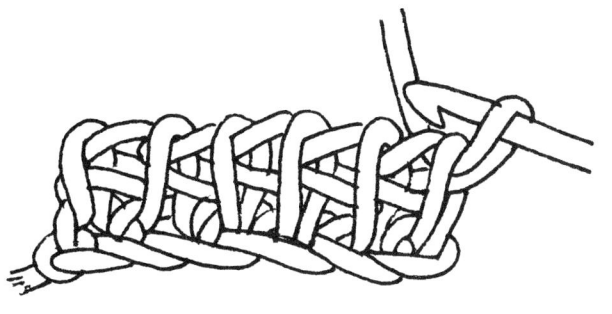
Tunisian crochet, return row completed

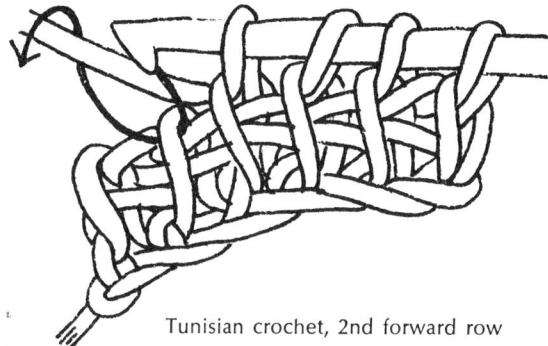
Tunisian crochet, 2nd forward row

TUNISIAN KNITTED CROCHET

The 1st outward and return rows are worked exactly as above. For the 2nd and all succeeding outward rows, insert the hook from the front through the horizontal loops of the stitches in the preceding row. The return rows are worked as in ordinary tunisian crochet.

The photograph shows how closely this kind of crochet worked from the front resembles ordinary knitting. It is, however, considerably stronger than knitting because of the firmness of the stitches.

Knitted tunisian crochet, forward row

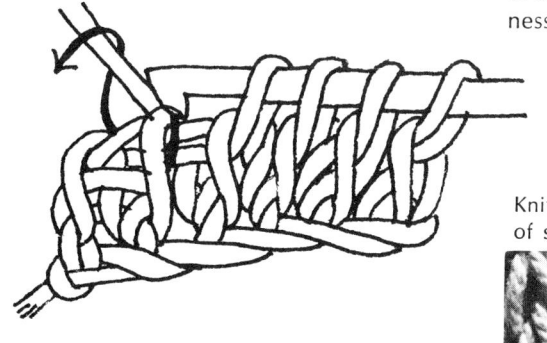

Knitted tunisian crochet resembles knitting because of its close rows of stitches

4.
IDEAS & PATTERNS

Opinions differ as to the way a crochet pattern should be presented. Some people like to follow a pattern stitch by stitch, others like to pick up the general idea at a quick glance and then work it out themselves in their own way.

This book tries to accommodate both alternatives, diametrically opposed to each other though they are. Complete technical instructions are provided for each model, so that once the manual technique of crochet has been mastered, the reader can start to work on the patterns. But at the same time each pattern exemplifies some fresh principle in crochet, and shows the variations that can be made on a given pattern, so as to open the way for those who prefer to work more freely.

Crochet is a technique in which it is easy to work without a pattern, freely and spontaneously. But, on the other hand, free crochet does not mean that anything goes. In the explanations of the following patterns it is frequently pointed out that if an idea is to be successful, some forethought will be necessary.

As to the sizes of crochet hooks recommended, these are included to give some guidance in relation to the yarn employed, but a margin of a whole size smaller or larger is easily allowable. The sizes suggested are only approximate. The material suggested will make a piece that looks like the one shown; however, other materials will make tighter or looser fabrics, each with its own individual texture. Remember that the sizes of hooks are given in millimeters, according to the new international numbering, and that a conversion table for the old numbering or lettering is provided at the back of the book.

FOUR CROCHETED BELTS

The belt in Pattern 1 is worked in a stiff, shiny string that is normally used by upholsterers. The belt in Pattern 2 is made of a strong, tarred twine obtainable in marine supply stores. Both these belts are fastened with old brass buttons.

The belt in Pattern 3 is made of strong fish-netting. Twine of this kind was used for making nets before the days of nylon. It is of unbleached cotton, and will stand the boiling water necessary for washing again and again. This belt is wider than the first two.

The belt in Pattern 4, which is fastened with a decorative brooch, is made of a linen warp thread used in weaving. Thin twine could also be used.

Pattern 1: String belt
Materials: upholsterer's string, or other twine, and a button
Hook: 6½
Work plan: simple 3-row belt with loop to close, about 36 inches (95 cm) around
Belt

Cast-on row: 80 ch and 1 ch to turn

2nd row: ss back along cast-on row, 1 ch st into the 1st cast-on ch st, so that you can work around it, because you will be working ss back along the other side of the cast-on row

3rd row: Put the hook into the row of ch st and not into the row of ss on the opposite side (see detail drawing). Make ss in each ch st

Belt Loop

At the end of the 3rd row, work a small loop of 4 ch, and fasten off by running the yarn in along the loops backward and forwards a few times. Sew a button on the other end after checking for length

Putting the hook into the row of chain stitches rather than the row of slip stitches. In this way you work around the cast-on row

Pattern 1: String belt

Pattern 2: Tarred-twine belt
Materials: tarred twine and a button
Hook: 7
Work Plan: simple 3-row belt, see directions for Pattern 1

Cast-on row: because the hook is larger the ch sts will be larger, and you must measure the length of the belt as you cast on

Succeeding rows: see Pattern 1

Pattern 2: Tarred-twine belt

Pattern 3: Fish-netting belt

Materials: fish-netting from a marine supply store, or other appropriately sized crochet cotton or twine, button
Hook: 7
Work Plan: this wider belt is made by adding a single additional row of ss to a belt like those in Patterns 1 and 2
  Cast-on row–3rd row: see Pattern 2
  4th row: ss into the back loop of 3rd row

Pattern 3: Fish-netting belt

Pattern 4: Linen warp-thread belt

Materials: linen warp thread, or thin twine, and a decorative clasp or brooch
Hook: 3
Work Plan: as this belt is fastened with a brooch and overlaps, length is not so important. The belt in the photograph is about 42 inches long and about 1½ inches wide (109 × 4 cm), and is made in the same general way as the others from 5 rows of ss and sc. When it is finished, the belt should be lightly pressed
  Cast-on row: 150 ch
  2nd row: ss worked in the front loop
  3rd row: ss worked in the front loop
  4th row: sc worked in the front loop
  5th row: sc worked under both loops

Pattern 4: Linen warp-thread belt

CROCHET WITH TWINE AND WOODEN BEADS

Around the middle of the last century, women frequently crocheted small bags and purses with beads. Often quite complicated color patterns were carried out in the beadwork, and the creation of these small works of art must have been no small labor. First the beads had to be strung onto fine crochet thread, in the proper color sequence for the pattern, and, after that, care had to be taken to work in one bead with every stitch that was made.

If you work with coarse yarn and wooden beads instead of glass beads and fine yarn, you can make bags and crocheted bands quite quickly. Bands can be crocheted to the exact length and width required, and before you know it you have a finished article to wear—a belt or a hair band.

BEAD CROCHET

In bead crochet, the beads always lie at the back of the work. Only if you crochet in the round can you get the beads to lie close together, side by side, in each row. If you work in single crochet, the beads will lie on the slant. If you work in half-double crochet, they will lie straight, that is, with the holes upward in relation to the direction of the work.

The beads must be threaded onto the yarn first, and then each bead must be pushed down into the stitch in the preceding row to ensure that it will lie firmly.

The two bands shown in Patterns 5 and 6 easily can be used for belts. The slight stiffness of the material gives them the necessary firmness, and, as the beads catch when the belt is lightly tied around the waist, no other form of fastening is required.

In bead crochet, the beads must be threaded onto the yarn first, and each bead must be pushed firmly down into the stitch in the preceding row

Pattern 5: Narrow beaded band

Materials: tarred twine, 130 wooden beads of two shades in 7mm diameter (about ¼ inch)
Hook: 4½
Work Plan: a five-row belt, worked around the cast on row as in Patterns 1-4, with beads worked in on the last round
    Cast-on row: after threading 130 beads, work 130 ch
    2nd row: 3 sc in same st, sc for rest of row, 3 sc in same st to turn
    3rd row: sc, close round with ss
    4th row: sc, work in bead with every other st
    5th row: sc, work in bead with every other st

Pattern 5: Narrow beaded band

Pattern 6: Wide beaded band
Materials: tarred twine, 150 beads
Hooks: 4½
Work Plan: a five-row belt like Pattern 5, measuring about 50 inches (130 cm)
   Cast-on row: after threading 150 beads, work 150 ch
   2nd row: joined h dc
   3rd row: joined h dc
   4th row: ss, work in bead with every other st
   5th row: ss, work in bead with every other st

Pattern 6: Wide beaded band

It is neither difficult nor troublesome to crochet with beads provided that a coarse yarn is used and correspondingly large beads are threaded into the stitches

Pattern 7: Shoulder bag of tarred twine
Materials: coarse tarred twine
Hook: 6½ or 7
Work Plan: start from the bottom, and work the sides up from this. Turn the bag inside out, as it will keep its shape better this way. Work the strap separately, and sew or crochet it on. The material is coarser than that used for the belts, and will withstand wind, weather, and hard wear. It may come a little hard at first to work with such stiff twine; take care not to draw the stitches too tight, and keep your fingers relaxed

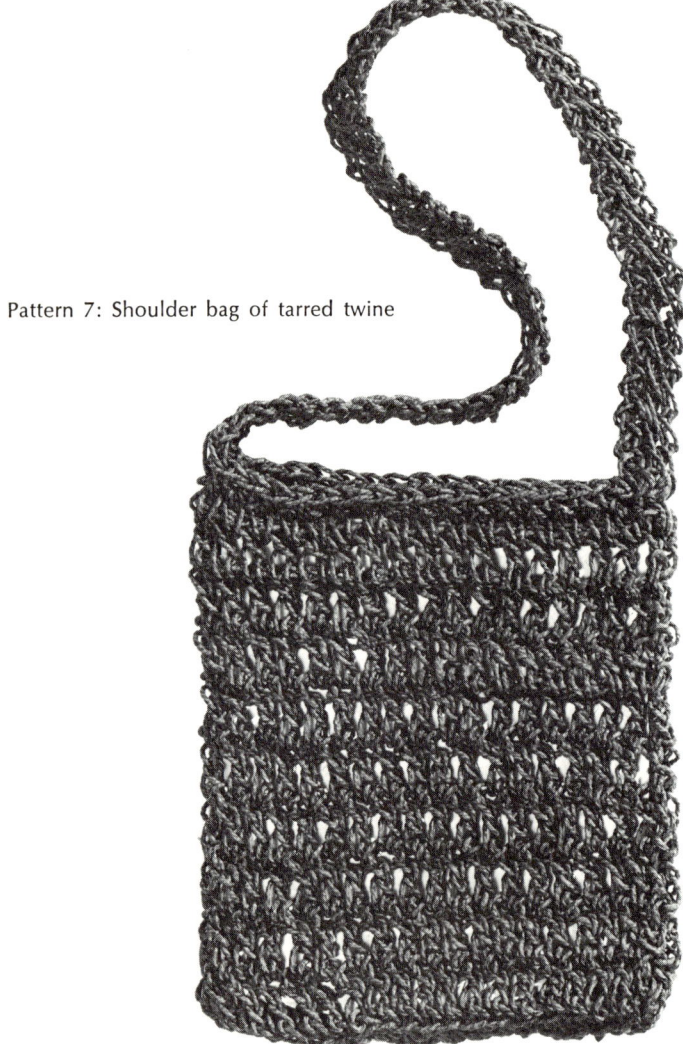

Pattern 7: Shoulder bag of tarred twine

Bottom

Cast-on row: 18 ch with double twine

2nd row: sc, 2 sc in same st at end of row to turn

3rd row: sc, close with ss (this round of 2nd and 3rd rows has 38 sts in all)

Sides

4th–9th rnds: 2 ch (which equal the height of 1 dc), dc under both loops

10th and 11th rnds: sc (this makes the edge firmer)

Fasten off the bag by splitting the yarn, after which you can knot the two ends together over one of the threads in a stitch and weave backwards and forwards with each of the split strands

Strap

Cast-on row (tunisian crochet): 3 ch. Put the hook in the 2nd ch, draw 1 loop onto the hook. Put the hook into 1st ch and draw 1 loop onto the hook. This completes the forward row with 3 loops on the hook

2nd row (return): make an over, draw yarn through 1st loop. Make an over, draw through the first 2 loops, make an over, and draw through the last 2 loops

3rd row (forward): put hook in 1st space (see drawing) and draw a loop onto the hook; then put hook into next space, etc. until there are 3 loops on hook

4th row (return): same as 2nd row

Succeeding forward and return rows: work as in 3rd and 4th rows until strap is required length

Finish bag by sewing strap on at both ends. You can also crochet it on by working the strap continuously from the last rnd of the bag, and merely have to fasten the other end by sewing

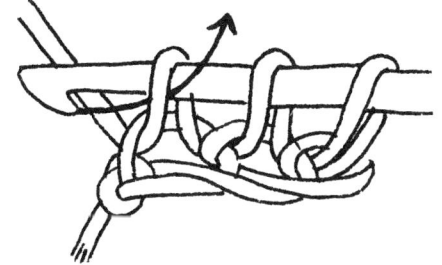

The strap in Pattern 7 is made from a 3-stitch row of tunisian crochet

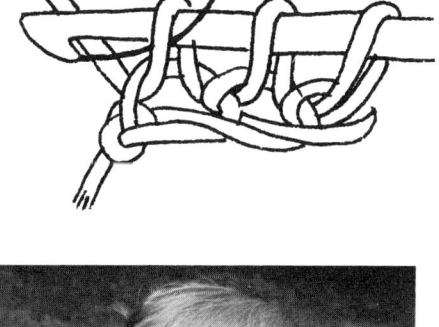

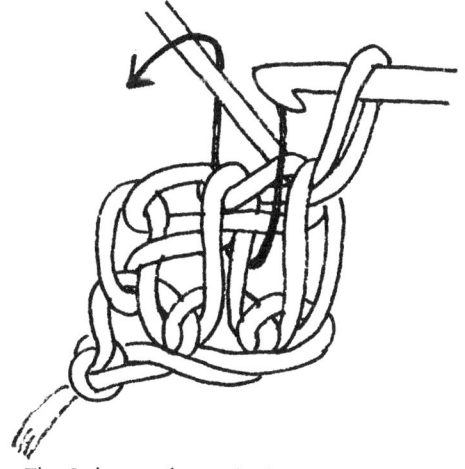

The 3rd row of strap in Pattern 7 is a variation of the forward row in tunisian crochet

Continue working the strap in Pattern 7 until it is the required length

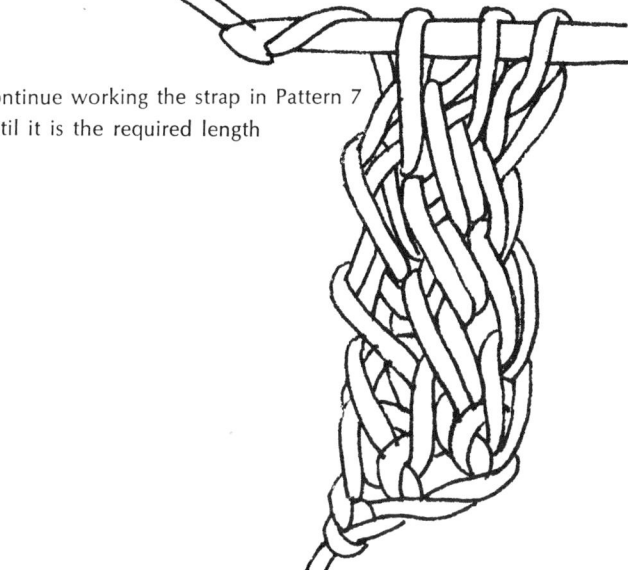

A tarred-twine shoulder bag is light to carry on a country walk

JOINING-ON AND CHANGING YARN: RUG IN STREAKS OF COLOR

Yarn must be changed when a pattern calls for varied colors or, in a large project of a single color, when one skein runs out. You can change in a number of ways, either at the end of a row or in the middle.

WEAVER'S KNOT

A weaver's knot is designed to take up the least possible space and give the greatest possible strength. It is a practical knot for crochet, and with a little practice you can tie it in a second.

Cross the ends of the yarn and hold them between the thumb and forefinger of the left hand. Bring the yarn up over the thumb and under and over the crossed threads. Now bring the loose end on the right over and under the yarn, moving the left thumb so that it holds firm the two threads that lie parallel in the drawing. At the same time, pull the thread (marked in the drawing by an arrow) with the right hand. The last drawing shows the finished knot.

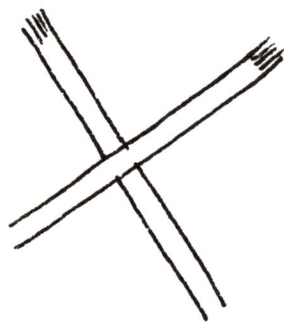

Weaver's knot, step 1

Weaver's knot, step 2

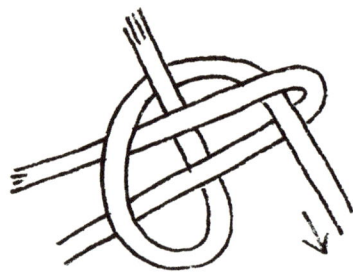

Weaver's knot, step 3: pull on the end marked by the arrow

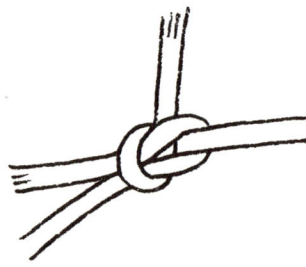

Weaver's knot, completed

CHANGING YARN BY WORKING IN SINGLE CROCHET

If you do not tie a knot you can leave the two ends of the yarn loose for about 4 inches, and work them in later with the stitches by weaving them backwards and forwards.

You can also change the yarn by crocheting a little way over the end of the new yarn. Then insert the hook into the loop, pick up the new yarn, and continue working normally. The next few stitches are worked over the end of the "old" yarn, in order to hide the join.

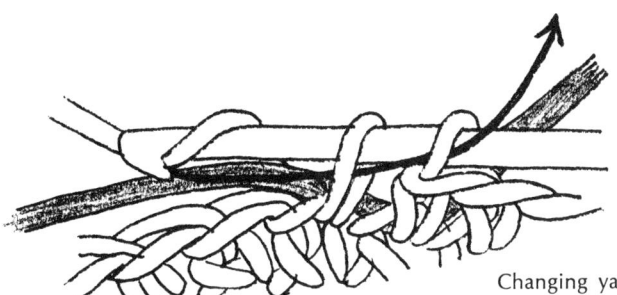

Changing yarn by crocheting over the end of the new yarn, step 1

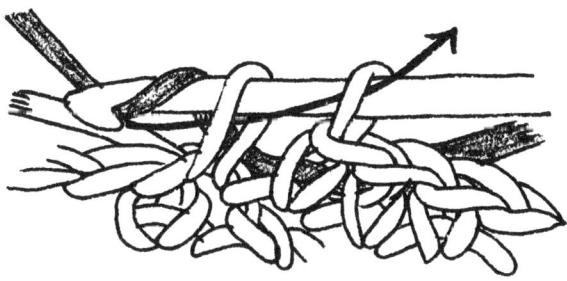

Changing yarn by crocheting over the end of the new yarn, step 2

CHANGING YARN BY WORKING IN DOUBLE CROCHET

Owing to the height and looser structure of the double and higher stitches it is not possible to hide the ends of the yarn by working over them, so that a different method has to be used.

Make an over and insert the hook into the loop as usual. Pick up both ends of the yarn, both the new and the old, and draw them back through the loop. Make an over with the end of the new yarn, and draw it through the double loop and the next single loop on the hook. Make an over, and draw through the 2 loops remaining on the hook.

Changing yarn in double crochet or higher stitches

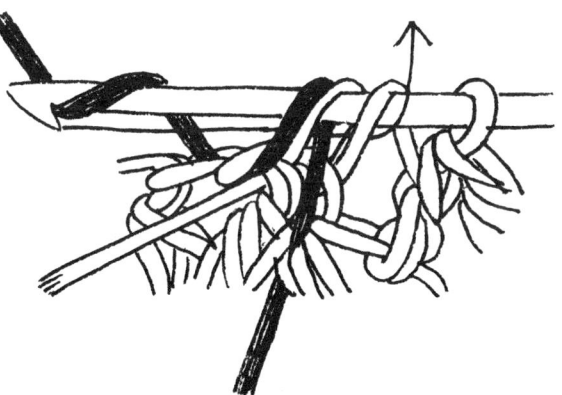

LARGE RUG IN STREAKS OF COLOR

In the large rug shown here, worked in rya wool, a number of short lengths of different colors of yarn were employed, necessitating frequent joining-on. A project such as this can be much less costly if you use yarn remnants. Keep your eyes open for opportunities to buy odd lots of yarn. Weaving and spinning mills and carpet factories sometimes offer remainders for sale. These are often in colors and materials that you cannot buy in the usual retail outlets. Such odd lots may be offered for sale because they are in shades that have gone out of production, or they may be short ends of yarn that are no longer useful for industrial purposes, although they are perfect for use in handcrafts. The price reduction has nothing to do with the quality, which is usually first-rate.

This rug was worked in single crochet from a number of short ends of yarn from a carpet factory. The colors are shades of flame red, orange, yellow, sulphur, ice blue, and brown. These available shades and the particular softness of the material suggested the idea of fire to me, and from that the pattern evolved. Possibly memories of a recent visit to Mount Etna in Sicily played their part, and the combination of colors suggests fire and sulphur vapours, and fire in connection with earth.

Large rug in streaks of color. The glowing colors of this rug are shown in color plate 6 on page 4

The method of crochet was also evolved by the necessity of frequent changes of yarn. It was an advantage to work with 2 strands at the same time as the row could then start with two strands of the same color and, when one ran out, another of a different blending or contrasting shade could be worked in with the first.

By degrees, as the work proceeded, further purchases of yarn were made, in colors that supported the original idea. The quality of the new yarn was somewhat harder than the first lot, which helped accentuate the difference between the elements of the design.

Detail of the large rug shows the simple stitches worked in double strands of yarn

When working on a large article like this, it is best to sit on the floor. This ensures that the work is kept flat all the time. As the streaks of color could not always be continued for a whole row, but sometimes ran out in the middle and were picked up again with something different in the next row, forming a sort of a break, it was necessary to get up every now and then to judge the effect from a distance to decide how to go on. The very fact that the quantity of each color is restricted and that you have to make something out of the material available, can act as an inspiration in itself.

MATCHING HAT AND SCARF

This cap and scarf are easy to make, and the color of the stripes forms the pattern. The choice of colors is a matter of individual taste, but the model is worked in shades of green and yellow. The crochet hook is large compared to the yarn, which gives a light, airy fabric. Even though the cap is worked in the round and the scarf is worked to and fro, there is not enough difference in the stitch for it to be noticeable.

Patterns 8 and 9: Matching hat and scarf, also shown in color plate 12 on page 6

Pattern 8: Hat

Material: 2-ply weaving wool or other thin yarn
Hook: 7
Work Plan: work doubles inserted between doubles of preceding round (see drawings on page 34) and change colors after varying numbers of rounds. In the model: 4 rounds in green, 1 in olive, 1 in gray-green, 3 in yellow, 1 in gray-green, 1 in olive, 1 in green, etc.

Cast-on row: 50 ch, close in ring with ss

2nd–10th rnds: 2 ch, dc, inserted between sts in preceding rnd

11th rnd: 2 ch, dc (as above), inc in every 3rd st by working 2 sts in same st

12th–13th rnd: 2 ch, dc (as above), dec in every 3rd st by working 2 sts together

14th rnd: 2 ch, dc (as above), dec in every 4th st

15th–18th rnds: 1 ch, sc with 2 extra strands of yarn, for strength

Fasten off the loose ends, pull the cap into shape. As a finishing touch you can make a small tassel, using all the colors and sew it to the side of the cap

Pattern 9: Scarf (see photograph for Pattern 8)

Material: 2-ply weaving wool or other thin yarn
Hook: 7
Work plan: work doubles inserted between doubles of the preceding row, and use the same colors as in the hat

Scarf

Cast-on row: ch to the desired length of the scarf. In model 125 ch equals about 4 feet (125 cm)

Succeeding rows: 2 ch, dc, inserted between sts in preceding row

Finish off and work 1 or 2 rows dc into the cast-on sts to get the 2 sides to match

Fringe

To cover the ends, make a fringe at each end. First cut threads about 8 inches (20 cm) long. Then gather them into tufts of 5 threads (matching the colors of the different stripes they will be attached to). Double the threads over, and attach by means of a crochet hook, as shown in the drawing

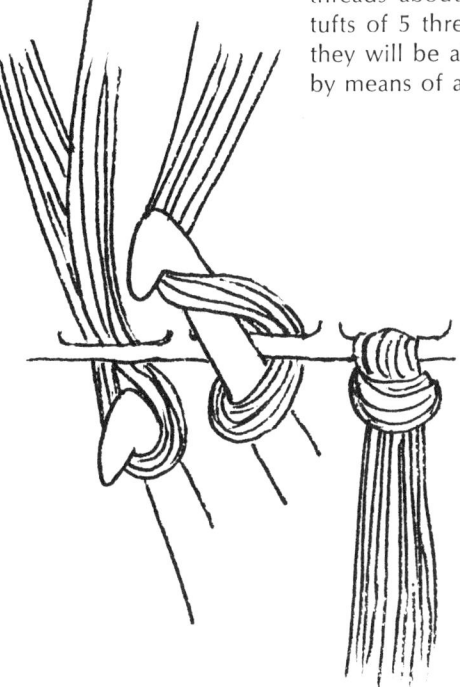

Making the fringe for the scarf in Pattern 9

PONCHO CAPES

A poncho is a very useful garment. It is easy to slip on over the head, and is attractive on both children and adults. The examples shown here are worked in the same yarn as Patterns 8 and 9, but the hook is much finer, which produces smaller stitches.

If you are making a poncho for a child, it is worth remembering that the poncho can grow with the child. It is not difficult to lengthen it—you merely have to work on 1 or 2 more stripes. It is worth remembering this when choosing the material. A poncho can last for years.

Pattern 10: Poncho in triple-triple crochet
Material: 2-ply weaving wool or other thin yarn
Hook: 4
Work plan: work in the round in narrow and broad stripes of varying colors. In the model: narrow stripes in white, light ochre, dark gray, and brownish tones (varied irregularly); broad stripes are all in medium gray

Poncho
 Cast-on row: 72 sc (a double ch), and close ring with ss
 2nd–8th rnds: 1 sc to begin, sc all along rnd, close with ss. Work each rnd in a different color. Inc in each rnd at center front and center back by working 3 sts into same center st
 9th rnd: ch to equal height of tr tr, tr tr all along rnd, 1 ss to close
 Succeeding rnds: repeat pattern of 7 rnds sc, 1 rnd tr tr, until desired length is attained

Fringe
The quickest way to cut the yarn for a fringe is to wind the yarn around a book that is about 6 inches wide (15 cm) and then cut the yarn through at one side. This quickly gives a quantity of threads about 12 inches long (30 cm). The fringe is made of tufts of 5 strands, all of the gray color. Double the threads over and attach them to the bottom edge at intervals of 1 stitch, as described in Pattern 9

Pattern 10: Poncho in triple-triple crochet

Pattern 11: Child's poncho (on left)
Material: 2-ply weaving wool or other thin yarn
Hook: 4
Work Plan: work as Pattern 10, but use triple crochet. Make a total of 5 stripes (7 rounds of single crochet, 1 round of triple crochet in each stripe). This should give a total length from neck to lowest point of about 22 inches (56 cm). Add a fringe of 8-inch threads, which will add another 4 inches (10 cm) to the total length

Pattern 12: Poncho with broad stripes in 3 colors (on right in photograph for Pattern 11)
Material: 2-ply weaving wool or other thin yarn
Hook: 6
Work Plan: work as Pattern 10, but use half-double crochet instead of triple-triple crochet. Each stripe is 6 rounds wide, and the 3 colors should alternate regularly. No single color should be dominant or brighter than the rest, which would give a disagreeable pattern effect. The increases are made in the center front and center back, as in the other ponchos

Patterns 11 and 12: Child's Poncho (left) and poncho in broad stripes (right). Not requiring a close fit, ponchos for an adult or child can be made from the same pattern by adjusting the length

FINISHING WITH EDGINGS, PICOTS, AND KNOTS

EDGINGS

To get the sides of a finished work even and tidy, it may be necessary to crochet an edging. This generally consists of 1 or more rows of single crochet. If the stitches at the side have been made too open or too loose, small adjustments can then be made by means of extra decreases. This sort of tidying up may be decisive for the final appearance and durability of the piece of work.

If an article has been worked from the same side all the time, the edge will lie more smoothly if the last row is worked from the other side.

Usually, 3 edging stitches are worked into the corner stitch to ensure that the corner lies smooth. This also prevents pulling.

PICOTS

If you prefer a decorative edge to an even one, there are various forms of picot edgings or small knots that can be used. The simplest form is an edging of loops of chain stitches that are drawn together at their starting points. The drawing shows 4 chain stitches, drawn together by a slip stitch. After the slip stitch, there are 2 single crochets and another loop.

A picot made from 4 chain stitches

A large picot edge may be worked as follows.
Cast-on row: 5 ch
2nd row: 1 sc in 4th ch, 1 h dc in 3rd ch, 1 dc in 2nd ch, and 1 tr in 1st ch. Secure last st with 1 sc, skip over whatever number of sts in the edge corresponds to the height of the dc
Repeat for next picot

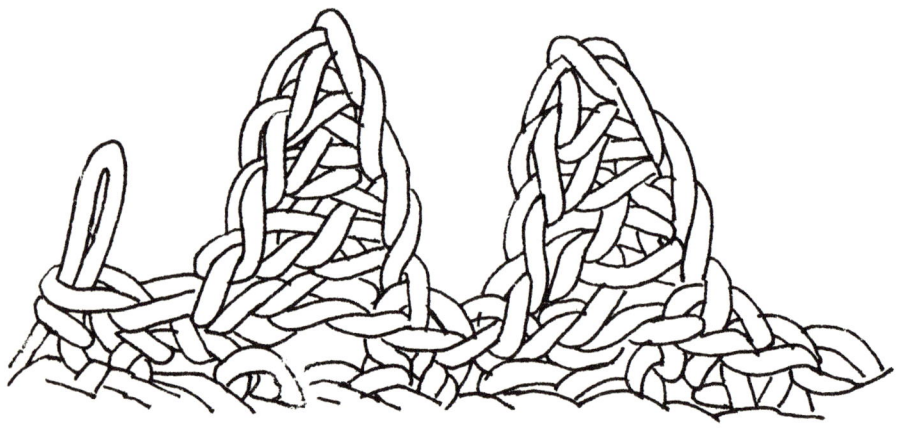

A large picot edging made from stitches of varying heights

A picot edging worked separately can be sewn onto the work so that the joining is almost invisible. You can make a picot edging before beginning the main body of the work, and use it as the cast-on row.

A separately made picot edge may be made as follows.
Cast-on row: 6 ch
2nd row: 1 dc in 2nd ch, 1 tr in 1st ch
Repeat for next picot

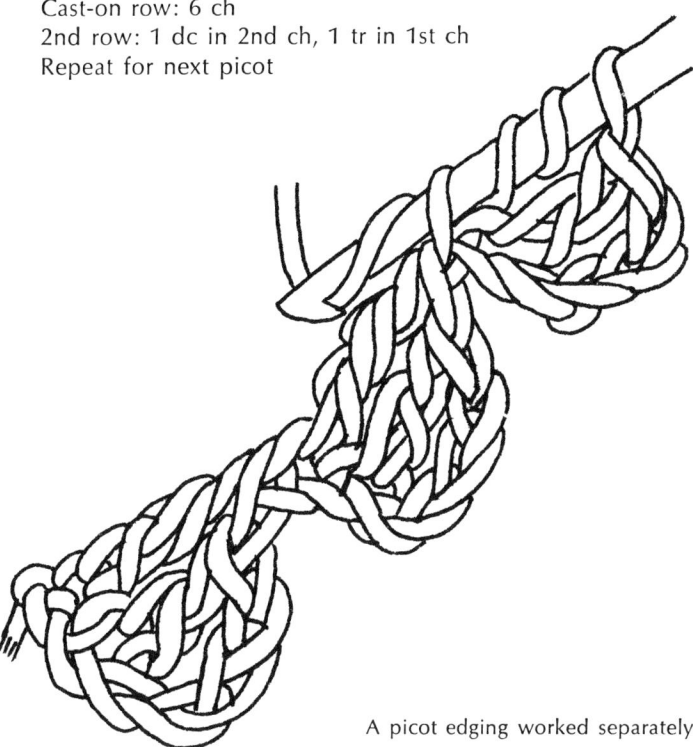

A picot edging worked separately

SECURED PICOTS, OR KNOTS

This form of picot is made by withdrawing the crochet hook after making the initial chain for the loop, putting it through the 1st chain stitch, picking up the free loop, and drawing it through the chain stitch.

For larger knots, work more chain stitches to begin. You must, in that case, increase the distance between the knots by skipping a greater number of stitches.

Secured picots, or knots, are made by withdrawing the hook after the initial chain is complete and picking it up after the hook is inserted in the first chain stitch

CROCHETED CORDS

A cord of the same material as the piece you are making is often required as a method of drawing the piece closed, or tying it in some way. It may also be useful to make cords for varying purposes. With crochet, they can be made as thick and strong as a strap or as thin and pliable as a string.

The simplest cord is an ordinary chain-stitch string, which can be made stronger by using a number of strands of yarn at the same time. A simple tie can be made with an extra row of slip stitches worked into the chain.

Chain-stitch cord using many strands of yarn

A crocheted cord can be made stronger by adding a row of slip stitches to the cast-on chain

MULTI-COLOR CORDS

A decorative effect can be produced by crocheting with 2 strands of yarn, each of a different color. Or you can crochet with these two different colors alternately. To do this, place both strands over the forefinger in the ordinary way, and then alternately pick them up and drop them, crocheting one chain with each.

Crocheting alternately with 2 different colors to make a chain-stitch cord

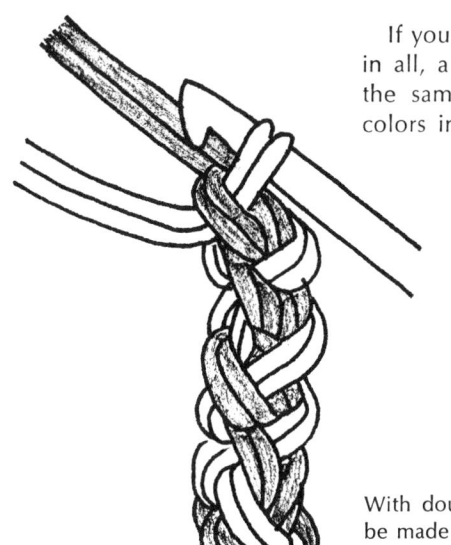

If you work with double yarn in each color, that is, 4 strands in all, a thicker cord will result. Or 3 colors can be used on the same principle, always taking care to use the different colors in the same order.

With double yarn in each color, 4 strands in all, a thicker cord can be made by crocheting alternately with each color

CORDS IN THE ROUND

A cord may also be made by crocheting in the round, with either 3 or 5-6 chain stitches in the ring. A thick cord will result from the greater number of chain stitches. If you use a strong yarn, the result will be a strap.

Here is a pattern for a simple cord.

Cast-on row: 3 ch, join in ring with 1 ss

Succeeding rnds: 1 sc in each st. Continue until you have reached the desired length

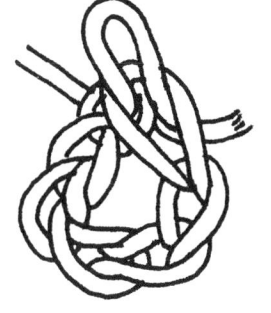

Crocheting a cord in the round, step 1

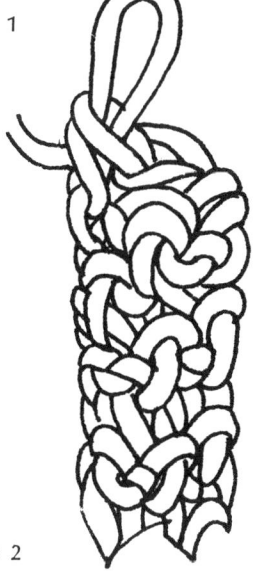

Crocheting a cord in the round, step 2

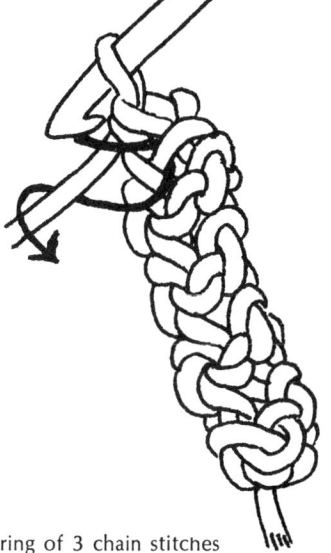

A cord crocheted in the round from an initial ring of 3 chain stitches

Pattern 13: A rug that turns into a cape
Material: thin 2-ply weaving yarn, or other thin wool, used 3 strands at a time. If you are buying yarn specially to make a rug like this, and want to avoid having scraps of too many different colors left over, here is an example of how to calculate the quantities you will need of each color. The rug is striped in 4 colors. One of them predominates and is used also as the outline, or border. Altogether there are 88 rows of stitches. If you make 4 rows of each color before switching to the next, you will use 16 rows before repeating your color pattern. By repeating this color unit 5 times, you will use 80 rows, leaving you 4 rows at the beginning and 4 rows at the end for the main color (80 + 8 = 88). You will need 300 grams (or about 11 ounces) of each of the 3 subsidiary colors, and 900 grams (or about 32 ounces) of the main color, which is also used for the 4 rows at the beginning and end and for the edging at the sides

Pattern 13: A rug that turns into a cape. This "transformation" rug is ideal for traveling and picnicking

Hook: 6½ or 7

Work Plan: the ordinary rug shown in the photograph has two slits in it for your arms to go through when you put the "rug" around you like a cape. A crocheted cord is threaded through the long side of the rug, so that it can be gathered. When the cape is laid over the shoulders and the cord is drawn tight, the cape falls in soft folds from the neckline. For the sake of symmetry, a corresponding cord is threaded through the other side. A decorative tassel at each end of the two cords prevents them from slipping through

In the model, the rug is about 48 inches wide and about 60 inches long (120 × 150 cm). Light stripes alternate with dark stripes in several shades of brown and blue

Rug

   Cast-on row: 115 ch, 3 ch to turn

   2nd–13th row: dc, inserted under both loops (use this form of dc in all rows)

   14th row: 24 dc, 24 free ch, which are attached after skipping 24 sts with dc, continue dc to end of row. This forms the slit for one arm

   16th–73rd row: dc

   74th row: make a slit for the other arm, as in 14th row

   75th–88th row: dc

Edging

   1st rnd: sc. On the two long sides work 2 sc to the height of each dc. Work 3 sts in each corner st

   2nd rnd: secured picots (see page 61)

   The slits are also edged with picots along the side that will lie uppermost

Cords

   Work 2 cords in the round, using 3 single crochet stitches closed in a ring as the base. When the cords are about 60 inches long (150 cm), thread them through the outside row of double crochet, under 2 stitches and over 2 stitches. Sew tassels to the ends

Slits for the arms in Pattern 13 are made in the 14th and 74th rows. A cord is threaded through each side—one is the functional one for the neckline drawstring, and the other is for symmetry

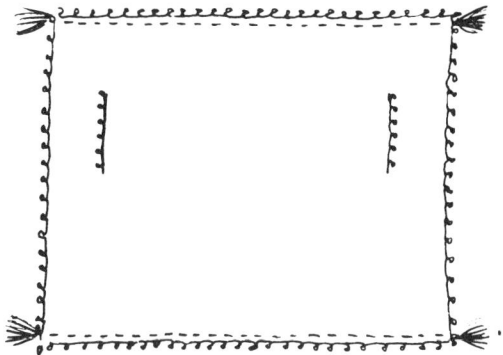

The rug in Pattern 13 is a cape when worn over the shoulders and drawn closed at the neckline with a crocheted cord

CROCHET IN SQUARES AND CIRCLES

Two pot holders serve as models for crocheting in simple geometrical shapes. They are large enough to be used as mats for warm dishes as well as for holding pots and kettles. Both the square and the circle are started from a closed ring of chain stitches.

Pattern 14: Square pot holder
Material: Mayflower cotton No. 8 or other ordinary crochet cotton, used 3 strands at a time
Hook: 3½
Work Plan: work in the round until the pot holder measures about 8¼ inches in width (21 cm). No hanging loop is necessary because the picots that form the edge can be used for hanging. Except for the last round, the single crochet stitches are worked in the back loop of the stitch, which makes each separate round stand out very distinctly
  Cast-on row: 4 ch, close with ss
  2nd rnd: 1 ch, 3 sc in each of the 4 ch (to form the corners), close with 1 ss
  3rd–16th rnds: 1 ch, sc in each ch, 3 sc in each of the center sts of the corners. This gives an increase of 8 sts in every rnd
  17th rnd: For the straight sides, work sc under both loops. For the corners, work 10 ch from the 1st corner st and attach with 1 sc, 10 ch from the 2nd corner st and attach with 3 sc in the same st, and 10 ch from the 3rd corner st and attach with 1 sc
  This edging may be worked in a different color from the body of the pot holder

Pattern 14: Square pot holder

Pattern 15: Round pot holder
Material: Mayflower cotton No. 8 or other ordinary crochet cotton, used 3 strands at a time
Hook: 3½
Work Plan: work in the round in a spiral until the pot holder measures about 8¼ inches in diameter (21 cm). To do this, do not close each round with a slip stitch, but mark the starting point of each round by looping in a little piece of thread. Use single crochet worked into the back loop, except in the last round where it is worked under both loops for strength. In the model three colors were used, 2 for the body of the pot holder and 1 for the picot edging
  Cast-on row: 4 ch, close with 1 ss
  2nd–3rd rnds: 2 sc in each st
  4th rnd: alternate 2 sc in each st with 1 sc
  Succeeding rnds: In each rnd, inc the space between each inc by 1 st. For example, use 2 sc in same st, 1 sc in next 2 sts; then 2 sc in same st, 1 sc in next 3 sts. Do not follow this pattern too closely, for if too many inc are made, the edge will ruffle, and if too few are made it will draw. A feeling for the correct number of inc will come with practice, and is good preparation for free crochet
  Last rnd: count the number of sts you have, and divide them into 12 groups—6 for the picot grouping, and 6 for the straight edging in between. In the model: 6 picots of 10 ch each, attached by 1 sc, then 8 sc in both loops before the next picot grouping

Pattern 15: Round pot holder

CASTING-ON IN A RING THAT CAN BE DRAWN CLOSED

If you wish to use a large number of stitches in the innermost, or first round, here is a method by which you can cast on any number of stitches, and then gather them into a ring that can be completely closed by drawing up the loose end of the yarn.

This method lets the material determine how many stitches there should be in the cast-on ring, and therefore is important when crocheting without a pattern.

Place the yarn as shown in the drawing, and then put the hook into the circle *from underneath*. Draw a loop onto the hook. Now work as many single crochet stitches onto the ring as desired, by working around the yarn that forms the ring. When you have the necessary number of stitches, pull the loose end of the yarn tight, and close the ring with a slip stitch.

Start the next round with the number of chain stitches that correspond to the height of the stitch you will be using in the next round.

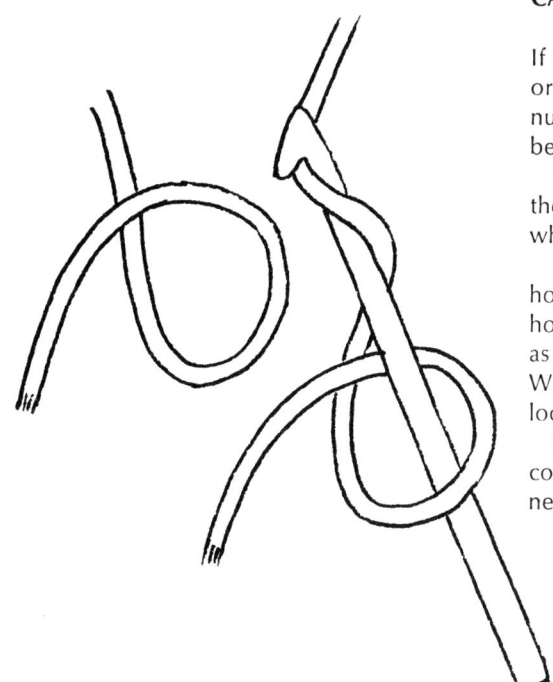

Casting-on in a ring that can be drawn closed, step 1

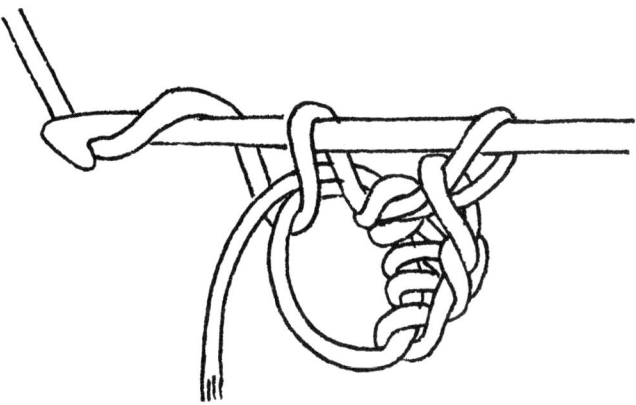

Casting-on in a ring that can be drawn closed, step 2

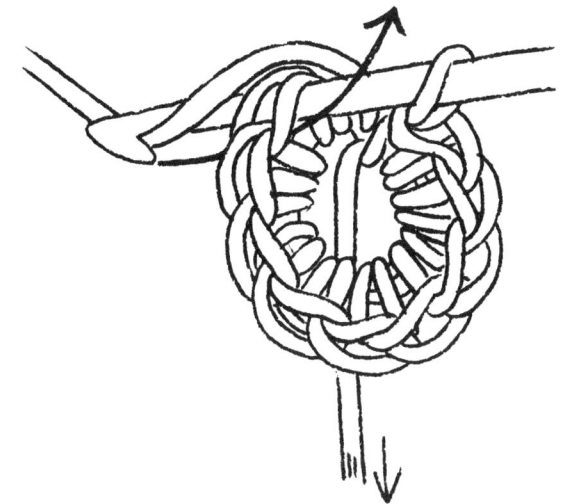

Casting-on in a ring that can be drawn closed, step 3: when required number of stitches are made, pull on the end marked by the arrow to draw the ring together

CIRCULAR SHAPES IN SISAL

Sisal yarns can be obtained in a wide range of thicknesses and are excellent for any article that must take hard wear. Sisal is good for round mats to set hot dishes on and for baskets and cushions to be used out of doors, perhaps for sitting around the barbecue, in the garden, or at a summer house (see Patterns 17 and 19). The natural buff color of sisal yellows with time but, if you prefer, you can easily dye sisal with cold-water powder dyes, as shown in the flat cushion in Pattern 16.

Sisal is a versatile yarn for many articles in crochet. A round mat for serving from hot dishes can be made by following a pattern similar to Pattern 15

Pattern 16: Flat sisal cushion
Material: sisal yarn or other heavy twine
Hook: 9
Work Plan: make two circular shapes of about 16 inches (40 cm), place a sheet of foam rubber in between, and sew the sides together. Work a loop for hanging, and attach. The front and back are each worked as in Pattern 15
Front
  Cast-on rnd: 12 dc in ring that can be closed, 1 ss
  Succeeding rnds: dc, inc by working 3 sts in center st of each corner
Back
  Repeat directions for the front
Hanging Loop
  Work a chain of the required length, and then work back along it in ss. Attach to one end of the sewed-up cushion

Pattern 16: Flat sisal cushion

CYLINDRICAL SHAPES IN SISAL

This waste-paper basket and the garden basket in Pattern 17 are much simpler to make than they appear. Begin with a flat circular or rectangular shape, similar to those used in Patterns 14 and 15. The cylindrical shape is built up from this flat shape merely by *not* increasing in the rounds used for the sides.

The transition from bottom to sides is best effected by crocheting into the back loops in the round that marks the edge of the bottom. With this type of stitch, the stiff yarn cannot hold the stitches flat, but throws them forward. If, at the same time, you stop increasing, the sides will rise straight up.

Both the baskets are worked on the same principle, beginning with 14 double crochets worked in a ring. The waste-paper basket, worked in thinner sisal with the same-sized hook, has a row of edging slip stitches where the handles for the garden basket begin.

Waste-paper basket in sisal. This can be made by varying the garden basket in Pattern 17

68

Pattern 17: Strong garden basket of sisal

Material: thick sisal yarn or other very heavy twine

Hook: 9

Work Plan: start with a flat circular shape, work up the sides by not increasing, and work the handles into the last round

Cast-on rnd: 14 dc in ring that can be drawn closed, 1 ss

2nd rnd: 2 ch, 2 dc into each st

3rd rnd: 2 ch, h dc

4th rnd: 2 ch, 2 dc into each st

5th rnd: as in 3rd rnd

6th rnd: 2 ch, h dc worked into the back loop, which forms a very definite edge

7th–11th rnds: 2 ch, h dc without inc

12th rnd: 2 ch, dc without inc

13th rnd: turn the basket inside out to get the particular striped effect on the outside, and work in joined h dc without inc

14th rnd: 24 ss, 10 ch, skip 9 sts to the right and remove hook from loop on chain to insert it into this st. Draw loose loop through, to fasten ch to edge again. Work ss into the ch st loop to complete the first handle. Work ss around the edge to the opposite point and make the other handle there in the same way

15th rnd: ss worked in the opposite direction

Pattern 17: Strong garden basket of sisal, also shown in color plate 10 on page 5

SMALL MAT AND DECORATIVE CUSHION IN SISAL

The tough sisal yarns are perfect to make articles for people who like to sit or lie on the floor. The crocheting can be quite hard work, but if you sit on the floor and relax thoroughly, right down from the shoulder, you should be able to complete each piece in just a few hours.

Pattern 18: Small mat in sisal

Material: 3-ply sisal yarn
Hook: 9
Work Plan: the center of the mat is worked to and fro in rows, and then the border is worked in the round. Final dimensions are approximately 32 × 36 inches (80 × 90 cm)

Cast-on row: 28 ch, 2 ch to turn
2nd–15th rows: dc worked into the front loop

1st rnd: 2 ch, dc, 3 dc into each corner st, 1 ss to close
2nd rnd: 2 ch,*1 ch and skip 1 st, 1 dc*. By repeating this pattern, you form a row of holes. In the corner sts: 1 dc, 4 ch, 1 dc
3rd rnd: sc (into both dc and ch of preceding row)
4th rnd: sc worked in opposite direction (by turning the mat over)

Pattern 18: Small mat in sisal

Pattern 19: Decorative cushion in sisal

Material: 2-ply sisal yarn or strong string
Hook: 6½
Work Plan: a square piece of crochet work is laid diagonally over a cushion and sewn together as shown in the diagrams, forming a pattern of decorative stripes. The square measures approximately 19 inches along each side (50 cm sq.), and the cushion should measure about 13 or 14 inches square (35 cm sq.) If you cannot find a cushion of this size, you can cut your own from foam rubber

  Cast-on row: 42 ch, 2 ch to turn
  2nd–21st row: dc worked into the front loop

Pattern 19: Decorative cushion in sisal

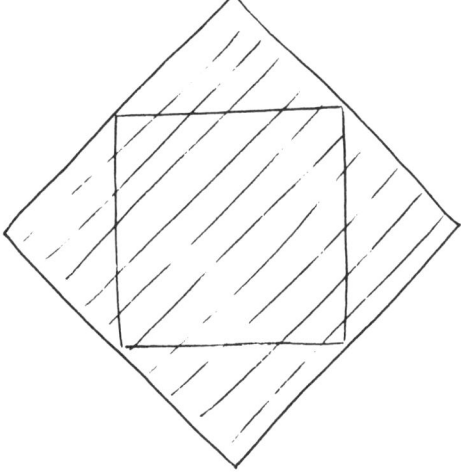

The cushion in Pattern 19 is covered by wrapping the crocheted piece around it on a diagonal

After the cushion in Pattern 19 is wrapped on the bias, it is sewed firmly together

IRREGULAR CIRCLE SHAPES

In the two common ways to make circles—ending each round with a slip stitch and working continuously in a spiral—the goal is to make a symmetrical form. In the following models, the circles are deliberately made a little lopsided so that it will not be necessary to keep to a regular number of stitches all the time, and also because a slight irregularity or variety is more interesting to look at than completely regular shapes, which can be better produced by machine.

The principle in making these irregular circles is that each new round or ring of the circle consists of stitches of differing heights, producing a slightly asymmetrical effect. In Pattern 20, exact directions are given for one of the circles in the rug to show that one can quite well have a definite system to start from, a system with which individual variations can be used to evolve a number of other interesting shapes.

It is not difficult to apply this principle on your own account to make irregular circles such as those used in Patterns 21 and 22. You merely have to remember that in increasing for a flat circle, the height of the different stitches plays a part. For example, in a round worked in single crochet, you will not need to increase as frequently as in a round in double or triple crochet.

A number of cushions based on variations on the theme of spiral crochet can look attractive together. See color plate 3 on page 3

SPIRAL CROCHET IN THREE COLORS

A pleasing irregularity of pattern can also be achieved by varying the colors in a spiral design, as in Pattern 23. To work a distinctive pattern in a spiral shape you have to have at least 3 colors going at the same time. At first this gives you the feeling that you are doing nothing but changing from one yarn to another, but this will ease as the spirals grow, and the distances between the changes of color increase.

It is also exciting to see how, with the help of differing heights of stitches, you can shape the streaks almost like sharpening pencils, making the point longer or shorter by using low single crochet stitches and then changing to half-double crochet and double crochet. You can then move on to triple crochet and from these work gradually back to the lowest kind of stitches.

A number of cushions based on these spiral designs can look attractive together, but they must not be identical. Once you have worked a spiral cushion and found the "melody," it is not difficult to vary the shape and size of the spiral in other cushions.

Pattern 20: "Knee-warmer" rug of irregular circle motifs
Material: 2-ply weaving wool or other thin yarn in 6 colors.

Pattern 20: "Knee-warmer" rug of irregular circle motifs, also shown in color plate 5 on page 4

You will need about 100 grams (approximately 4 ounces) of each of the 2 main colors and 25 grams (approximately 1 ounce) of each of the 4 subsidiary colors. In the model: half of the 20 squares have light gray-green circles on a darker gray-green background (these are the 2 main colors) and the other half have various distribution of the 4 other colors of light red-orange and ochre on a background of light gray-green
Hook: 4

Work Plan: this small rug, measuring about 34 × 40 inches (85 × 100 cm), is made up of 20 circle motifs in squared-off backgrounds. Sew them together by alternating single-color circles with multi-colored ones. After joining them, iron the work lightly, and then crochet a striped border in the 2 main colors. Detailed instructions are given for 1 of the multi-colored circles in the 4 subsidiary shades of light red-orange and ochre. The distribution of these colors should be varied in the other 9 multi-colored circles

Multi-colored circle motif

Cast-on rnd, 1st color: 12 dc in ring that can be drawn closed, 1 ss

2nd rnd, 1st color: 3 (2 sc in same st), 3 (2 h dc in same st), 3 (2 dc in same st), 3 (2 tr in same st). You now have worked a rnd of 24 sts of differing heights

3rd and succeeding rnds, *1st color:* 4 tr into 1st sc, 2 h dc, 15 sc; *2nd color:* 1 sc, 1 h dc, 2 h dc in next st, 3 h dc, 2 h dc in next st, 3 dc, 2 dc in next st, 4 dc, 2 dc in next st, 5 dc, 2 dc in next st, 10 (5 dc, 2 dc in next st); *3rd color:* 9 (5 sc, 2 dc in next st), 4 h dc, 2 h dc in next st, 3 (4 dc, 2 dc in next st), 3 h dc, 2 dc in next st, 3 h dc; *4th color:* 10 (5 sc, 2 sc in next st), (10 dc, 2 dc in next st), 5 sc

With this, you have completed the circle. The number of sts in the final rnd is 68. The square background shape in light gray-green is worked by dividing the 68 sts in the circle into 4 groups of 17 sts each. The center ones of these are worked with higher sts to form corners

1st rnd of background: Begin in the middle with 4 sc, 4 h dc, and 3 dc in the corner st. From here, start the next side portion of the square with 4 h dc, 8 sc (4 + 4 sts), 4 h dc and 3 dc in the next corner st. Continue this way until all the sides have been worked, and close with 1 ss

2nd rnd of background: 1 ch, work each side counting from corner, as follows—3 dc in corner st, 3 h dc, 12 dc (6 + 6 sts) 3 h dc, and you are ready to inc in the next corner

3rd rnd of background: dc with sc into each corner st

Single-colored circle motif

Use the same pattern of stitches as for the multi-colored ones, but work all in the same light gray-green color, until you come to the background, which is worked in dark gray-green. It may be a little difficult to follow the pattern, but you can keep count by, for example, laying a few match sticks in front of you and moving one match each time you have worked a set consisting of 5 sc, 2 sc into the next st

Border

Stripes in an irregular alternation of colors and of rows of different kinds of stitches are made. Use the 2 gray-green shades of yarn, and make rows of dc, h dc, and sc. In the model there are 12 rows in the border

Pattern 21: Square cushion with irregular circular motif
(on right in photo)
Material: 2-ply weaving wool or other thin yarn
Hook: 3
Work Plan: work in an irregular pattern of your own, as described in this section. The model is mainly in double crochet

Pattern 22: Rectangular cushion with irregular circular motif
(on left in photo)
Material: 2-ply weaving wool or other thin yarn
Hook: 4
Work Plan: work in an irregular pattern of your own, as described in this section. The model is worked in rounds that often have one side of the circle in single crochet and the other half in double crochet, with the transition stitches between them in half-double crochet. Because of this, each row stands out more distinctly. The border is not made in the round, but is worked to and fro in rows

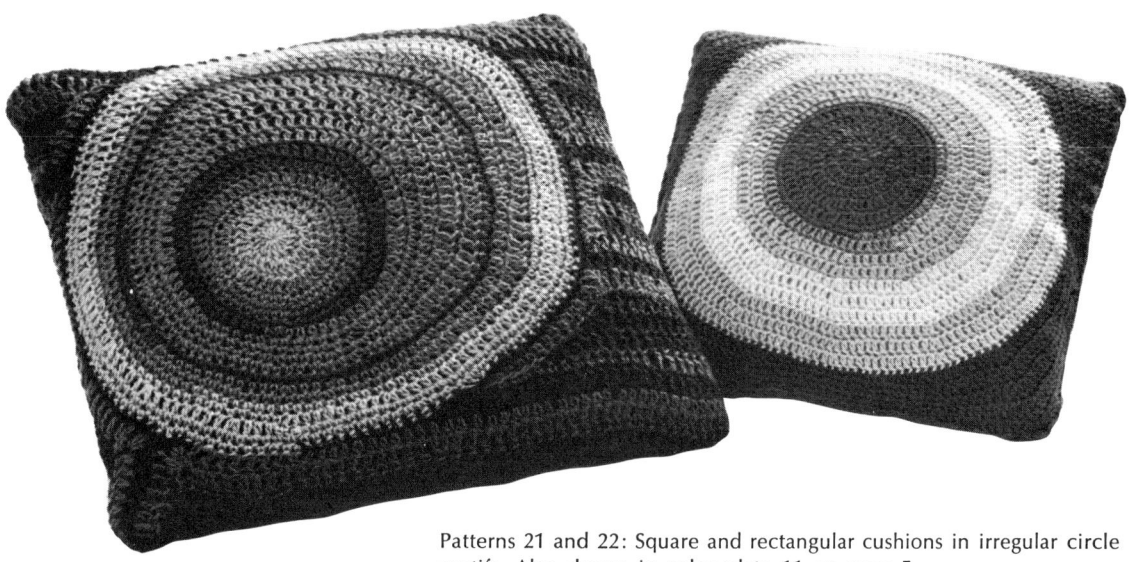

Patterns 21 and 22: Square and rectangular cushions in irregular circle motifs. Also shown in color plate 11 on page 5

Pattern 23: Cushion in spiral crochet
(on left in photo on page 76)
Material: rya wool, or rug wool, in 3 colors, a light, a dark, and a contrasting shade
Hook: 4½
Work Plan: the front, sides, and back are worked continuously in a spiral pattern, as described in this section, by increasing, working straight, and decreasing. A hole is left for a cushion to be stuffed into this cover, and then a small lid piece is made separately to close this hole

The diameter of the top is about 13 inches (33 cm). If no round cushion can be found to fit this, you can buy a square cushion approximately 14 inches wide (35 cm) and fit it into a cover made of 2 circular pieces of cotton about 12 inches in diameter (30 cm), before placing it into the crocheted cover

Patterns 23 and 24: Cushions in spiral crochet. Pattern 23 is at left, Pattern 24 is at right, and the cushion at the back is a free adaptation of the same kind of spiral

Top

Cast-on rnd, *light color:* 12 dc in a ring that can be drawn closed, 1 ss

2nd rnd; 2 ch, 2 dc in same st all the way around. Do not close the rnd, and continue with 3 h dc. Pull the loop of the last st out long, so there will be no need to pick at and fray the worked stitch later on, and continue with

the contrasting color: 2 (3 sc, 2 sc in next st), 2 (3 h dc, 2 h dc in next st), draw last loop out, and continue with

the light color: 2 (3 sc, 2 sc in next st), 2 (3 h dc, 2 h dc in next st), start here with

the dark color, beginning where the contrasting color ended: 2 (3 sc, 2 sc in next st), 2 (3 h dc, 2 h dc in next st), 2 (3 dc, 2 dc in next st), and work again with

the contrasting color: 6 (3 dc, 2 dc into next st), then

the dark color: 4 (3 dc, 2 dc in next st), then

the contrasting color: 4 (4 dc, 2 dc in next st), 5 dc, 1 h dc into the last st, 5 h dc, 1 sc into the last h dc, 5 sc, closing the round with this color. Continue in

the dark color: 10 (5 dc, 2 dc in the next st), 5 dc, 1 h dc in the last dc, 5 h dc, 1 sc in the last h dc, and cast off

Continue working the background in dc in a new color, or one of the first 3 colors, until the diameter measures 13 inches

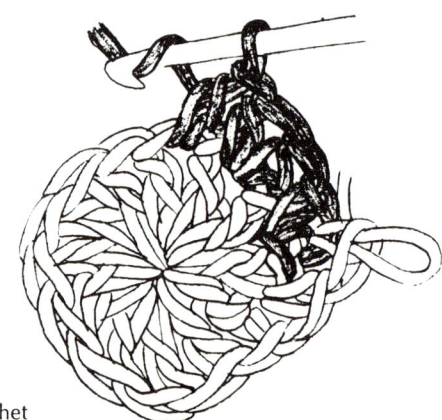

Joining-on a different color in spiral crochet

Side

1st rnd, in a different color from the background of the top: dc without inc, worked from the back around the post in the preceding rnd. Worked in this way the stitches will lie at right angles to the stitches in the preceding rnd

2nd rnd: repeat 1st rnd of side, so that another sharp edge will be formed

Back

1st rnd: like the last rnd of top

2nd–4th rnd: work by decr at the same rate as you inc in the last rows of the top

Lid

Repeat directions for the beginning spiral on the top, until you have a spiral piece that will cover the hole through which you stuffed in the cushion. Close the spiral, and sew it in firmly to the bottom piece, all around the edge of the hole

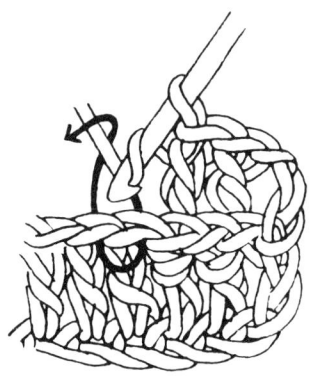

Working from back to front around the post to make the next row of stitches "turn the corner"

Pattern 24: Cushion in spiral crochet

(on right in photo on page 76)

Material: rya wool, or rug wool in 4 colors

Hook: 4½

Work Plan: work this on the same principle as Pattern 23, except that where the spiral stops on the top part of that cushion continue a different spiral, as directed below, in a completely different color or in a different shade of the dark color

1st rnd: 5 sc, 1 h dc into the last sc, 5 h dc, 1 dc into the last h dc, 5 dc, and repeat all around

2nd rnd: 5 dc, 2 dc into the next, or 6th st, repeat

3rd rnd: 6 dc, 2 dc into 7th st, repeat

4th rnd: 7 dc, 2 dc into 8th st, repeat

5th rnd: 8 dc, 2 dc into 9th st, repeat

When the top is the proper width, continue as for Pattern 23. The cushion at the back of the photo on page 76 shows an altogether free adaptation of the same principle used in the cushions for Patterns 23 and 24

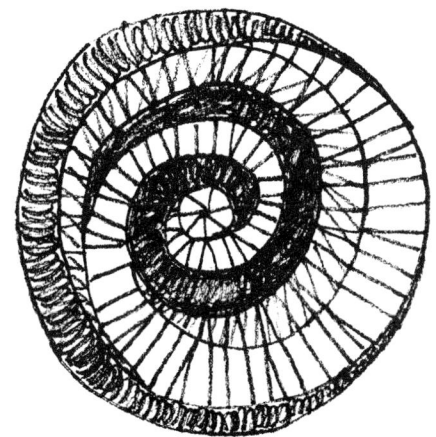

Diagram of the spiral. The photograph on page 76 shows a dark streak where there is a light streak here, but the alternation of colors is the same

FILLING IN AN OUTLINE IN FREE CROCHET

WORKING FROM A PAPER PATTERN

Very attractive articles can be made by following the form of a paper pattern in crochet. To make the work easier, use joined round or square motifs for the greatest part of the area, and then crochet around the edges to fill in the shape.

Make the pattern too small rather than too big, because you can always add rows or rounds of crochet. Join the large pieces as you work, to keep control of the different elements. Fasten all loose ends and iron the piece lightly when you are ready to lay out the piece on the pattern. It is a good idea to try on the article, if it is a garment, from time to time to make sure it fits.

Always work the background from the same side, because turning would drag the pieces too much. If necessary, stop and finish off, or possibly sew the pieces together a little way, if this is more convenient, before continuing another area of the background.

Pattern 25: Vest (waistcoat) in free crochet

Material: 2-ply weaving wool or other thin yarn, used in double strands

Hook: 4½

Work Plan: first prepare the paper pattern. Next, crochet 5 large and 8 small circles according to the directions for the multi-colored circle in Pattern 20. The small circles use only part of the pattern, the first and second colors, and the larger circles use all 4 colors. All the circles are edged, in a single color, in a picot pattern. The background stitches are up to you—this is free crochet

Paper Pattern

The drawing indicates the style of the vest. Each square corresponds to 10 cm (about 4 inches). With this as a basis, you can prepare your own personal pattern. Remember to make it a little too small rather than too large

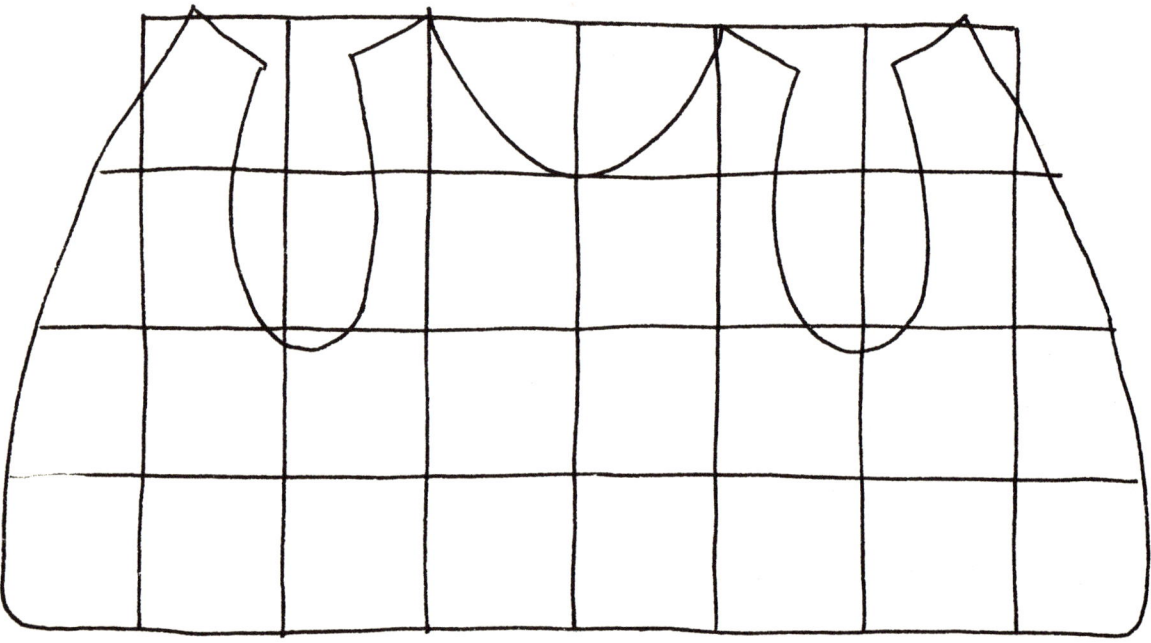

Paper pattern for Pattern 25. Each square equals about 4 inches. Remember to make your own pattern too small rather than too large, because additional rows of crochet can be easily added for adjustment

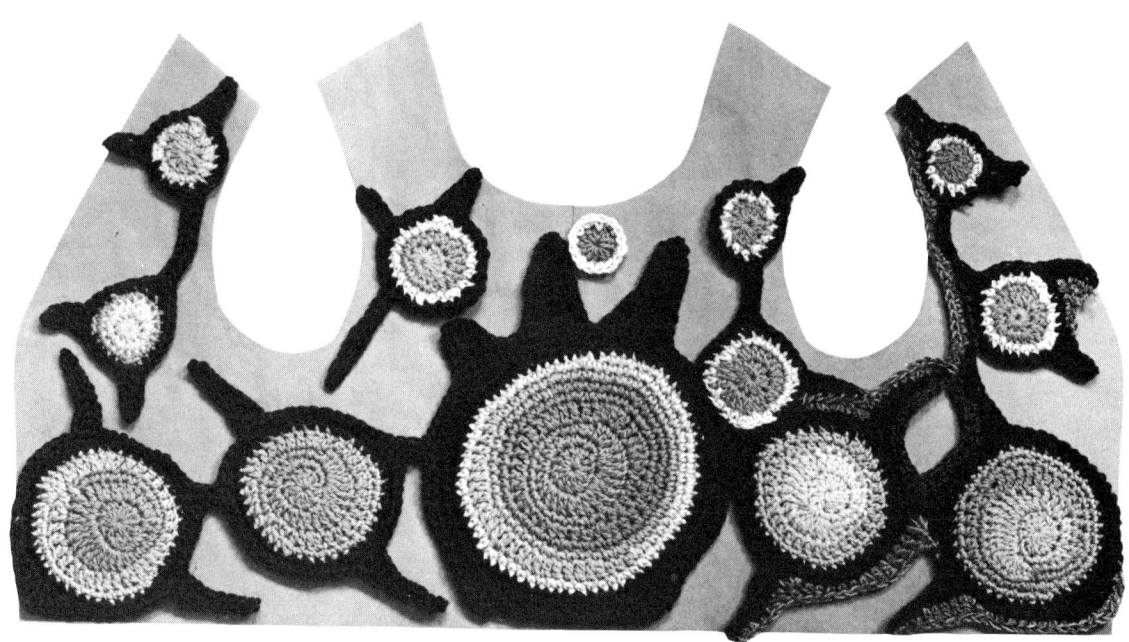

Laying out the circle motifs to fill the general outline of the paper pattern for Pattern 25

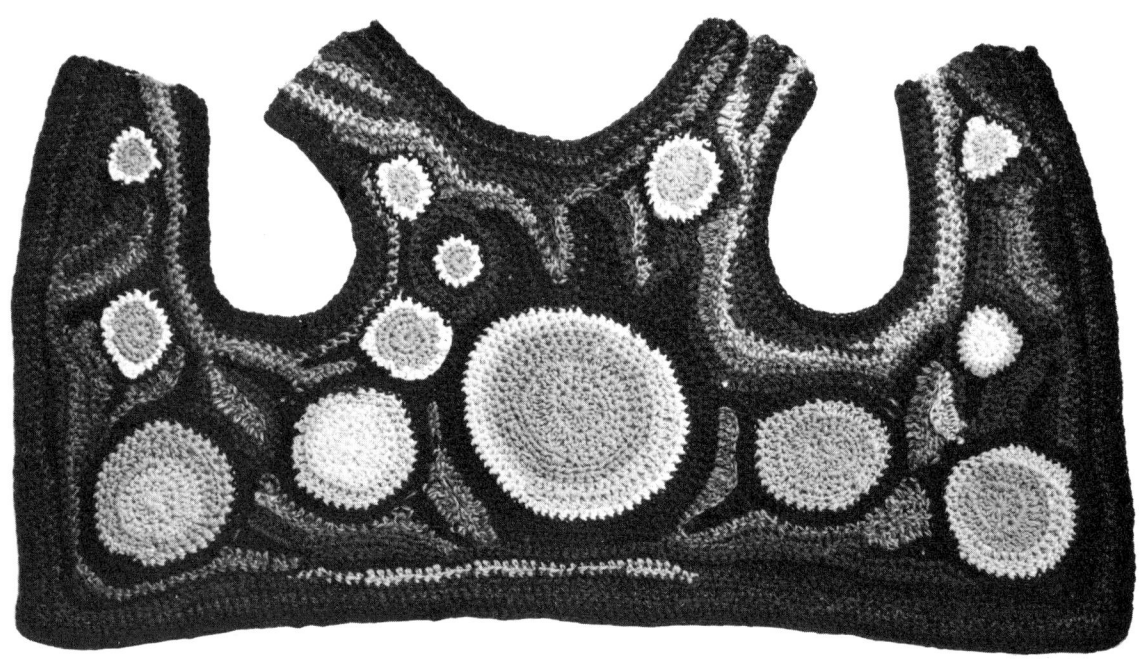

Pattern 25: Vest (waistcoat) in free crochet, also shown in color plate 1 on page 1. Only the shoulder seams have to be joined

Circle Motifs

The large circle at the center back is made with the full directions in Pattern 20. The medium circles are worked until they are about 4½ inches wide (11 cm), which allows for 2 colors. The small circles are started on the same pattern, but worked to varying sizes. The colors should be varied between them

Picot Edging in Leaf Pattern

Large Picot

Cast-on row: 10 ch

2nd row: 3 sc, 3 h dc, skip 2 sts from beginning of ch and attach to original edge

3rd row: (only for wider picot) 3 dc, 3 h dc, 2 sc, 3 sc in top st of picot, 2 sc, 3 h dc, 3 dc

Small Picot

Cast-on row: 5 ch

2nd row: 1 sc, 1 h dc, 2 dc

3rd row: (only for wider picot) as above, or all in sc

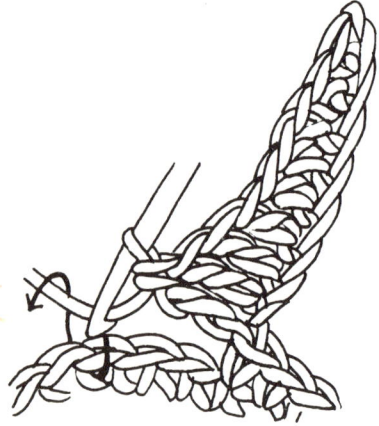

Large picot with 2 rows for edging circle motifs in Pattern 25

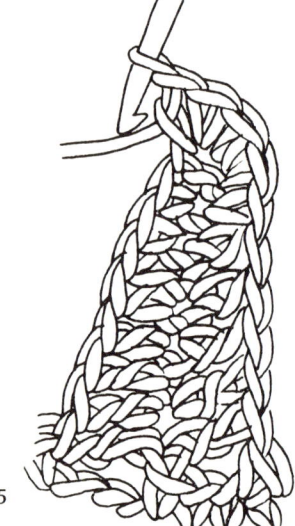

Large picot with 3 rows for edging circle motifs in Pattern 25

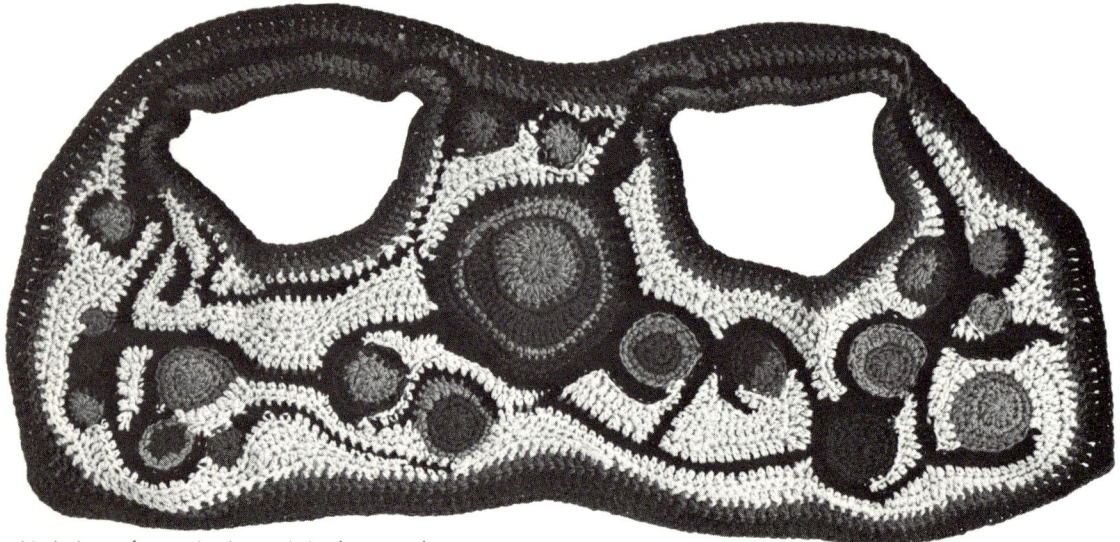

Variation of vest (waistcoat) in free crochet

WORKING FROM A NATURAL OUTLINE

A traveling bag lined with a lambskin is a good thing for a small baby when the winter is hard and cold. The shape of the bag is dictated by the natural shape of the lambskin, but the skin was cut away a little where it was too thin.

You may find other reasons for crocheting into a natural outline such as this, and it can be done on the same principle used in working from a paper pattern—connecting round or square shapes with strips or bands.

Shapes such as these can grow naturally by merely adding a few more rows or rounds of crochet. In order not to limit the life of this bag to the baby's first year, it is fastened with buttons, so that you can remove the buttons when the baby outgrows the bag, and use the bag as a rug.

Pattern 26: Baby's traveling bag lined with lambskin
Material: wooden buttons, lambskin, coarse rug wool, and soft hand-spun yarns for decorative effect. In the model: rug wool in browns and golds and natural wool in pale pinks, white, and shades of gray
Hook: 4½ for the rug wool, 8 for the natural wool
Work Plan: make a sufficient number of round shapes to fill the area of the skin, and then crochet around them to fill out the background. The stitches used are single crochet, half-double crochet, and double crochet

When finished, the cover is stitched to the skin at appropriate intervals, and the edge turned over and stitched down with strong thread. The loops for the buttons are worked in chain stitch

Detail of Pattern 26, showing the stitches used and the decorative effect achieved by varying the yarn

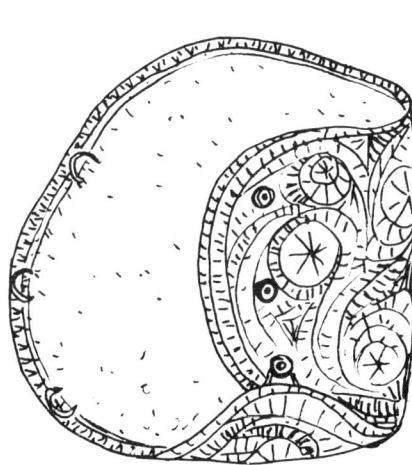

Pattern 26: Baby's traveling bag lined with lambskin, also shown in color plate 16 on page 8

After crocheting the outside of bag in Pattern 26, line it with lambskin as shown, and close with buttons and crocheted loops

Pattern 27: A large rug that looks like a space full of suns
Material: 2-ply weaving wool or other thin yarn
When starting on an ambitious project like this it is best to keep to one make of yarn, in which there are plenty of colors and shade variations available. In the model: circle motifs are in shades of yellow through orange to red. The background is in different shades of blue, giving an effect of spinning globes and suns in blue space
Hook: 4
Work Plan: the basics are similar to Patterns 25 and 26, but the plan for the free crochet is a more ambitious undertaking. There are many ways of tackling a rug like this, but for most people, the easiest is to start by crocheting the suns in different sizes and colors, and then lay them out to form a harmonious pattern. After that, they can be linked with a network of lines and curves running between them. Bring one sun in relationship to the next, and gather them all into a whole. Work quite spontaneously as regards shapes and colors, in simple stitches such as single crochet, half-double crochet, and double crochet

Pattern 27: A large rug that looks like a space full of suns, also shown in color plate 4 on page 4

A basic theme such as "a space full of suns" will help organize the colors and designs. Grouping the colors of yarns, all the greens, all the blues, etc., will help you quickly select the right shade to express your idea

It is the sort of job for which you will probably find it most comfortable to sit on the floor, not only to keep the rug flat, but to keep an eye on the pattern as it grows

Detail of Pattern 27. The rug is worked spontaneously in single, half-double, and double crochet

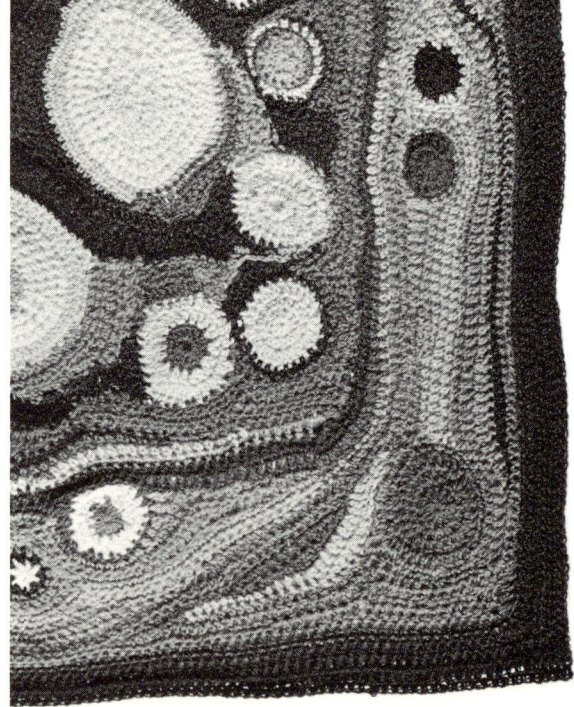

DECORATIVE BANDING AND FLOWER SHAPES

In many museums you can see samplers of patterns in knitting, needlework, and crochet. It is sometimes a good idea to practice these old patterns, so as to be able to incorporate them later into your own work. Such samplers can be mounted diagonally on a cushion, or used in varied combinations for fancy shawls and caps.

Rows of different stitches are often used to create decorative banding. Various stitches in combination with various colors can create many pleasing patterns, some of them flower shapes.

Pattern 28: Hat in patterned bands

Material: rya wool remnants in 5 colors, or other medium-sized wool. About 3 ounces of wool is required (80g)
Hook: 4½

Work Plan: the pattern consists of 2 identical patterned bands, each consisting of 4 circular shapes which are crocheted so that the 2 middle ones form squares and the 2 outer ones form pointed triangles. These are sewn together along the arrows shown in the drawing. Those of the same shape are varied by different color combinations. The 2 bands are then crocheted together in different colored irregular stripes, the height of the stripes varying gradually from single crochet to triple crochet stitches. From the bands, which form the lower part of the cap, add rows and rounds with decreases until the crown is complete. An extra edge at the wide end (as shown in the photograph) may have to be made to adjust the fit

Square

Cast-on rnd: 12 dc, 1 ss to close

2nd rnd: 2 × 2 dc in same st, in corner st: 1 dc, 1 tr, 1 dc. Repeat all the way around

Pattern 28: Hat in patterned bands, also shown in color plate 15 on page 7

Triangle

Cast-on rnd: 12 dc, 1 ss to close

2nd rnd: 3 h dc, 3 h dc in corner st, 2 h dc, 3 h dc in corner st, 3 h dc, in corner: 1 h dc, 1 dc, 1 tr, next st: 1 tr, 1 dc, 1 h dc

Joining the Bands

Sew the 2 circles for each band together at one side, then sew the triangles to the circles. To crochet the bands together, start at one corner and work a dc into each stitch along to the opposite corner. This piece now forms the back. Work the front piece so that the dc lie downward, that is, work with the wrong side out. When both the bands have been crocheted together, cast off

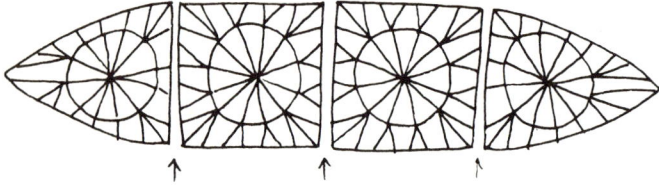

The square and triangular motifs in Pattern 28 are made from cast-on circles; each line in the drawing represents 1 double crochet

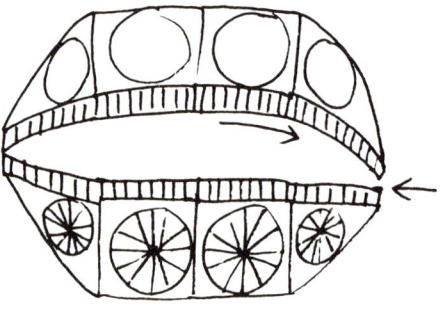

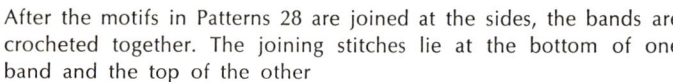

After the motifs in Patterns 28 are joined at the sides, the bands are crocheted together. The joining stitches lie at the bottom of one band and the top of the other

Crown

1st rnd; different color: dc around upper part of joined bands

2nd rnd: sc, making 5-6 dec

3rd rnd: h dc, about 25 sts in back half, change colors, 35 sts along the front. Adjust number of sts to individual fit

4th row, front only (see asterisk on drawing): h dc

5th row, front only, starting from same point as 4th row, but in different color: join into dc on back band 5 dc, 5 h dc, sc up to center front, from there work the same number of sc, 5 h dc, 5 dc, which are fastened to the dc row on the back band

6th row (working back): 2 dc, 2 h dc, sc for balance of row, end with 2 h dc, 2 dc

7th and 8th rows, different color: repeat 5th and 6th rows

9th rnd, different color: h dc, about 50 in whole rnd. If necessary, make dec

10th rnd, different color: dc with 5 dec (45 sts)

11th rnd: start 4 sts from center back and work 3 sc, 5 h dc, 5 dc with 1 dec, 5 tr with dec in 1st and 5th st, 5 dc with 1 dec, 5 h dc, then h dc with 2 dec until round is completed

12th rnd: 5 sc, change color, 4 h dc with 1 dec, 4 dc with 1 dec, 4 tr with dec in 1st and 4th st, 4 dc with 1 dec, 4 hlf dc with 1 dec

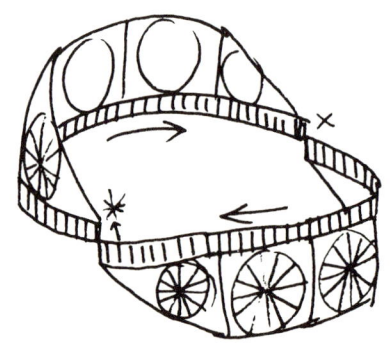

Making the crown of the hat in Pattern 28. Start the 4th row from the asterisk, and make decreases in successive rounds

13th rnd, different color: dec in every 3rd dc
14th rnd, different color: dec in every 2nd dc
15th rnd, different color: dec in every dc, then fasten off

Edge

Press cap lightly and, if necessary, crochet an edge around the lower, wide part of cap to adjust fit

Pattern 29: Cushion with diagonal stripes in fantasy stitch, pineapple stitch, and shell stitches

Material: rya wool or other rug wool
Hook: 4½
Work Plan: alternate rows of simple stitches with decorative stitch rows, and edge the piece with a border of single crochet around the sides. The sampler is 19 inches square (50 cm). Then cover a cushion of about 13 inches square (35 cm) by sewing the edges of the sampler together as shown in the drawings. Use a zipper along one side if you want the cover to be removable

The rows alternate as follows: 10 rows of double crochet in same color, 6 rows of fantasy stitch in 2 colors, 4 rows of single crochet in same color, 4 rows of pineapple stitch in different colors, 4 rows of single crochet in same color, 3 rows of shell stitch in 2 colors, 4 rows of single crochet in same color, 1 row of wound-shell stitch, worked alternately in 2 colors, 6 rows of single crochet in 3 different colors, 10 rows of single crochet in same color. See pages 36–41 for description of decorative stitches.)

Pattern 29: Cushion with diagonal stripes in fantasy stitch, pineapple stitch, and shell stitches

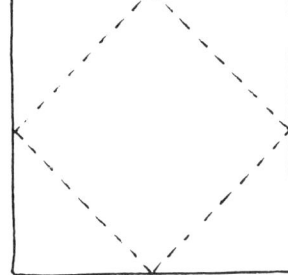

The cushion in Pattern 29 is laid on the cover in the space indicated by the dotted lines

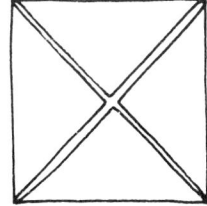

Then the cover is folded as shown, and sewn together. Use a zipper along the diagonal if you want the cover to be removable

Cast-on row: 52 loose ch sts

2nd–11th rows: 2 ch, dc

12th–17th rows: *fantasy stitch,* or joined single crochet, as follows. Begin with the light color. Start the row with 2 ch, put the hook in the 1st st and draw a loop up, then put it into the next st and draw a loop up, make an over and draw the yarn through all 3 loops on the hook. Then 1 ch. Repeat this group of sts, always inserting the hook the first time into the last st of the previous group. Change colors, make 2 ch to turn, insert hook into the 2nd turning ch, and draw a loop up. Insert hook into space formed between the groups in the preceding row, and draw a loop up, yarn over, and draw yarn through all 3 loops on hook. Then 1 ch. Repeat in this way all along row. In the next 4 rows, change color every row. This will repeat the double row 3 times, making 6 rows in all of fantasy st

18th–21st rows: 1 ch, sc

22nd–25th rows: *pineapple stitch* as follows. In the 1st row, work 3 ch to turn and 1 pineapple st into the 2nd sc in the preceding row. Make an over, put the hook in and draw a loop onto the hook, make an over, and draw through the first 2 loops, make another over, and draw through the 1st loop on the hook. Repeat this 6 times. Then make another over and draw a loop through the 6 loops on the hook. Make an over and draw the yarn through the last 2 loops, 1 ch, skip 1 st, and repeat the group all along the row. Use the same color for the next row, working 2 sc to each pineapple st all along. In the 3rd row of this pattern, use a different color, and work the first pineapple into the 2nd sc in the preceding row, which shifts the pattern along. Work the 4th row as the 2nd, using the same color and working 2 sc to each pineapple

26th–29th rows: 1 ch, sc

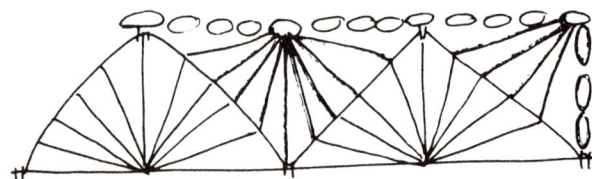

Shell stitch used in Pattern 29

30th–32nd rows: *shell stitch in 2 colors,* as follows. Work 1 sc into the 1st st, skip 2 sts, work 9 dc into the 3rd st, skip 2 sts, and repeat along the row. Change colors, and make 3 ch to turn, yarn over, and insert hook into the 1st dc of the preceding row, draw a loop onto the hook, yarn over, and draw through the 1st 2 loops, yarn over, and draw through the 1st loop on the hook. In this way, work 1 dc into each of the next 3 sts, so that finally there are 5 dc on the hook. Yarn over, and draw through all 5 loops at once. Draw the group together with 1 ch, then work 3 ch, and make 1 sc into the center st of the dc groups in the preceding row. Now make 3 ch and 9 dc in the same way as before, except that this time the shell is formed in the opposite direction, the half shell having been worked the first time. You must insert each of the 9 dc into a separate loop, not all in the same st as on the upward row. In the following sc row, work 1 sc into the gathering point of the shell sts in the preceding row, 2 sc into each of the ch sts, 1 sc into the center st of the next shell, 2 sc into the following ch sts, etc.

33rd–36th rows: 1 ch, sc

37th row: *wound-shell stitch* as follows. Using the first color, work 3 ch to turn, then 1 dc into the 2nd sc of the preceding row. Work a wound-shell stitch with 6 overs on the dc—make an over, go behind the dc and draw a loop onto the hook, repeat this 5 more times, yarn over, and draw the yarn through all the loops on the hook. Close the shell with a ch. Change colors, and skip 1 st in the preceding row before working another wound-shell stitch. Shift colors along the row

38th–43rd rows: 1 ch, sc. Alternate 3 different colors in this group of 6 rows

44th–53rd: 1 ch, sc. Use the same color for this group of 10 rows, as you used for the initial 10 rows

Edging

Work 2 rounds of single crochet all along the sides so that all the sides are the same length

Pattern 30: Flowered shawl

Material: 2-ply weaving wool or other thin yarn
Hook: 8
Work Plan: a simple shawl, made by increasing at the beginning of each row of half-double crochet. The wide, decorative border is made in a shell-stitch variation

Shawl

Cast-on row: 11 ch + 3 ch to turn

2nd row: 2 h dc in the 11th ch, skip 1 st, 2 h dc in next st, repeat along row. 3 ch to turn. This makes 6 groups of h dc

Pattern 30: Flowered shawl, also shown in color plate 2 on page 2

3rd–33rd rows: Work the next group of 2 h dc in outside loop of the 1st group of h dc (see drawing), then work the groups of h dc in the spaces between the groups in the preceding row. This produces 32 rows with an inc of 1 group at the beginning of each row. In the 33rd row of the shawl there will be 38 (32 + 6) groups in all

Border

1st rnd: joined h dc around all sides

2nd row: 1 sc, shell st (9 dc in same st) skip 2 sts, repeat along row

3rd row: joined h dc under each loop in the preceding row

4th row (reversed shells): 4 ch, 1 tr, 4 dc in next 4 sts, retaining the last loop of each on the hook. Draw last loop of the five loops on the hook through all, then make 5 ch and 1 sc in the point of the triangular shape in the preceding row. This 1st shell was a half. Whole shell: 5 ch sts, 9 dc as before, work off the 10 loops on the hook at the same time, 5 ch, sc in next point. Continue with whole shells, but end the row with a half shell

5th row (shells): 1st halfpoint starts in center of shell, 4 ch, 4 dc in same st, 1 sc in same sc as before. Continue with complete shells of 10 dc into the st that gathered together the dc in the preceding row

6th row: joined h dc as in 3rd row

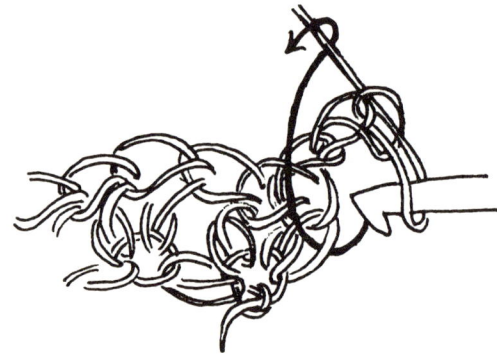

Making the increase for the shawl in Pattern 30 by working the half-double crochets in the outside loop

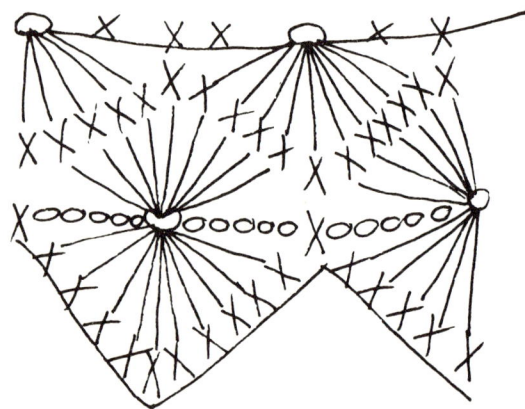

Last row of shells in Pattern 30, each containing 10 double crochets worked into the center stitch of preceding row

Pattern 31: Flowered cap

Material: 2-ply weaving wool or other thin yarn in different colors for each part of pattern. In model: various shades of black, gray, and white

Hook: 7

Work Plan: an adaptation of the shell pattern in Pattern 30, created with a hook that is large for the yarn, produces a lace-like effect. The cap is worked from the wide end upwards, and the decreasing is done by reducing the number of stitches that comprise each shell and the number of connecting stitches

Note that the color arrangement shown in the photograph is somewhat different from that given below. If you want this effect, work the 4th and 5th rows of the cap at the same time in the following way: work the 1st downward shell in one color, then work the 1st upward shell in the 2nd color over it. Work the 2nd downward shell in the 2nd color, and the 2nd upward shell in the 1st color, as shown in the drawing

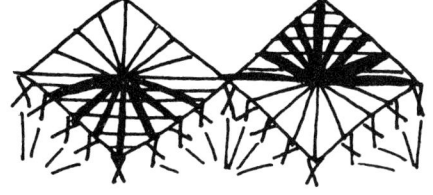

Shell stitch used in Pattern 31. Shells and reversed shells are combined with a variation in color

Edge

    Cast-on row: 50 ch with double yarn, close ring with ss

    2nd–3rd rnds: fantasy st (joined sc) as in Pattern 29

Cap

    1st rnd, different color: fantasy st

    2nd rnd: 3 ch, 9 tr in same st, skip 2 sts, 1 sc. Repeat along row so that there are total of 8 shells

    3rd rnd, different color: joined h dc into each of the tr of the previous rnd

    4th rnd, different color in downward shells: from top of triangle in previous row, work 3 ch, 9 tr retaining last loop on hook, work off at same time, 3 ch, 1 sc in next point

    5th rnd, different color in upward shells: 10 tr sts in center st of flower

    6th rnd, different color: joined h dc

    7th rnd: 5 sc into top st of point, 1 ch between points, repeat along row

    8th rnd, different color: 3 tr into space, gather together, 5 tr into sc, repeat along row

    9th rnd, different color: joined h dc

    10th rnd, different color: tr, finish off, and pull into shape

Pattern 31: Flowered cap, also shown in color plate 13 on page 6

Pattern 32: Summer cap in variation of flower pattern
Material: coarse linen thread in 2 contrasting colors. In model: white and dark blue
Hook: 6
Work Plan: a shell pattern similar to Pattern 31, in upward and downward shells, is worked from the lower edge up to the crown. The decrease is in the stitches that connect the shells. The edge is made after the cap is finished
Cap
  Cast-on row: 60 ch with double yarn in light color, close with ss
  2nd rnd: skip 1st 2 ch, 7 tr in 3rd ch, skip 2 ch, 1 sc in next st, skip 2 ch, 7 tr, etc. There should be 12 tr groups in all
  3rd rnd, dark color: 2 ch, attach with sc in center st of a shell, 1 tr in 1st tr to left of center st, and without drawing the yarn through the last 2 loops on the hook, work 1 tr, and work on in this way until there are 7 tr on the hook. Now yarn over and draw through all 8 loops, 2 ch, 1 sc into center tr of following shell. Continue this way along row
  4th rnd: work a shell of 7 tr in the st that joined the tr together in preceding rnd, 1 sc in sc in preceding rnd, repeat to end of rnd
  5th–6th rnds, light color: 5th like 3rd, 6th like 4th
  7th–8th rnds, dark color: repeat the shell pattern as above
  9th–10th rnds, light color: repeat the shell pattern as above
  11th rnd (or when the work measures about 8¼ inches or 21 cm), dark color: work downward half of pattern in dark color, finish off, and pull cap into shape
Edge
  1st–2nd rnds: double yarn in joined h dc
  3rd rnd: work in opposite direction in sc, which forms the distinct edge

Looked at from one point of view, the shells in Pattern 32 can be seen as rows of different-colored squares

Pattern 32: Summer cap in variation of flower pattern

Pattern 33: Cushion with flower heads

Material: rya wool or rug wool, in 3 colors. In the model the flowers are yellow and the circles are orange, edged with brown

Hook: 4½

Work Plan: the cushion cover consists of 42 yellow flowers, which are joined together at the corners. Then 42 orange circles are worked and joined to the flower heads as their brown edging is crocheted. Each flower is about 2¾ inches square (7 cm), and from this you can determined how many you will need to cover the cushion you have. Work around the cushion as you join the motifs

All the motifs are based on a cast-on ring that can be drawn closed. Always remember to draw this ring firmly together and finish the end by sewing back and forth on the back, so that the ring does not come open again

Flower

Cast-on ring: 20 dc, close with ss

2nd rnd: 2 ch, 8 dc worked into the same st from which the ch sts start, skip 4 ch, work 9 dc into the 5th ch. Work a total of 4 groups in this way. Gather the last group together with the first in a ss, and finish off

Crochet the flowers together as you work by linking the center dc in each group with the corresponding st in the next flower. The joining is done by withdrawing the hook from the loop of the st, inserting it from below through the corner st of the flower to be joined on, and from that picking up the loose loop, which is now drawn through as a ss

Circle

Cast-on rnd: 24 dc in a ring, close with ss, finish off

Edge for Circle (also joins to flower heads)

1st rnd: 1 sc, 2 ch. Then, with a ss, work around the joining of the 2 flowers, make 2 ch, go into the sc again with a ss. Then work 3 sc into each of the following dc in the ring. The joining point between 2 flower petals is connected, as before, with a ss. Again work 3 sc, 2 ch, and connect the next joining between flowers with a ss. Repeat all the way around, close, and fasten off

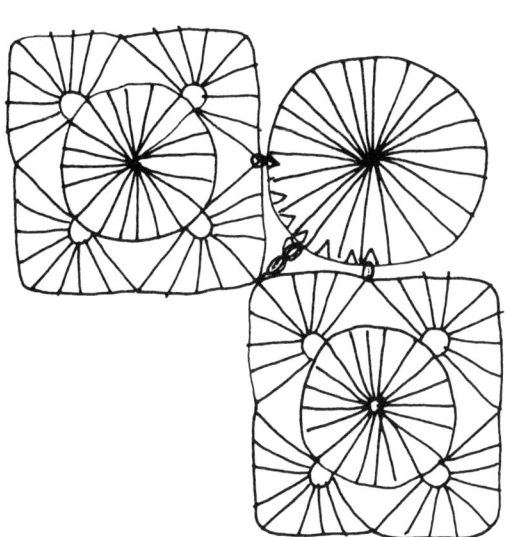

Connecting the separate motifs in Pattern 33

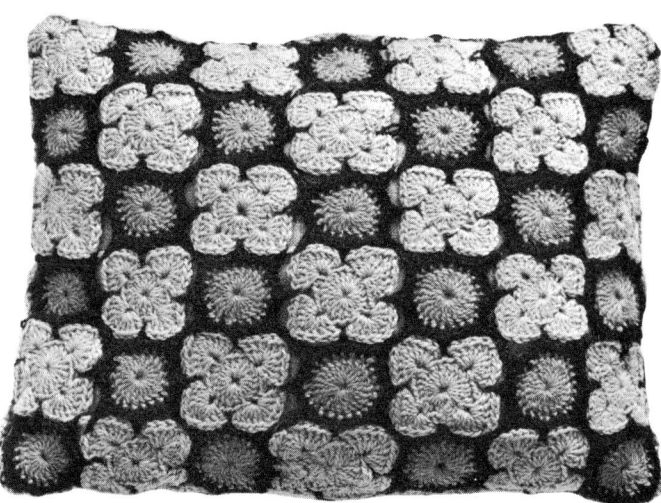

Pattern 33: Cushion with flower heads

ROSETTES AND FLOWER FIGURES

Open, lacelike crochet shapes were very much used in the last century for backgrounds, laces, and even entire bedspreads. Usually the shapes were worked symmetrically on a round central ring, and the figures could be divided into a number of loops or points divisible by 4, so that they could be incorporated in a square. These squares were then later stitched together to form larger units. In another, slightly freer form, which goes under the name Irish crochet or Irish lace the shapes are copied from old laces, and the rosettes and leaves of the figures are crocheted over a net background.

A few of these rosette shapes are shown on the following pages. Some, made in traditional crochet cotton, are worked over a foundation thread, which throws the form into stronger relief. The bag on page 95 is made in a much coarser material.

Motifs like these can be worked in various types of thread or yarn. The classical rosette patterns take on fresh life from new uses and new materials. Used alone, a single figure in unusual material can have a surprisingly decorative effect. For example, a small purse can be made dressier by adding a rosette with picot edging. Work this in a metallic yarn to stand hard wear and tear. Small flowers or small rosettes, possibly in different colors, can be stitched onto belts. A crocheted flower can be used on a child's shirt—or his pet—as one child did when the family tortoise calmly walked off into the tall grass. He stitched a bright rosette flower to 2-sided tape, and stuck it onto the tortoise's shell!

Pattern 34: Rosette with picot edge

Material: D M C yarn, or other crochet cotton. In the model highly pearlized cotton has been used to give a shiny effect
Hook: 3
Work Plan: work around a center ring formed of multiple loops of the yarn

Cast-on round: twist the yarn 24 times around your forefinger and next finger together, then work 36 sc around this ring, join with ss

2nd rnd: *6 sc, 8 ch, remove hook and insert at beginning of ch, draw loop through. Into the space made by the ch loop, make 3 sc, 1 picot, of 3 ch, and repeat this a total of 4 times, end with 3 sc*. Repeat between * a total of 6 times, to make 6 loops in all

Pattern 34: Rosette with picot edge

Pattern 35: Small rosette

Pattern 35: Small rosette
Material: pearlized DMC yarn or other crochet cotton
Hook: 3
Work Plan: to give a more pronounced shape, both rounds are crocheted around a piece of cord. If possible, use cord of the same color as the crochet yarn
   Cast-on rnd: make a loop of cord, and work 18 dc around it, close with ss
   2nd rnd, around cord: 1 sc, 1 h dc, 3 dc, 1 h dc, 1 sc, skip 2 sts, repeat so that there are a total of 6 loops

Pattern 36: Large rosette

Pattern 36: Large rosette
Material: pearlized DMC yarn or other crochet cotton
Hook: 3
Work Plan: on the same principle as the small rosette in Pattern 35, but without a cord
   Cast-on rnd: 24 dc in a ring, close with ss
   2nd rnd: 4 ch, skip 3 sts, 1 dc in 4th st, and repeat all the way around
   3rd rnd: into each ch st loop, work 1 sc, 1 h dc, 1 dc, 1 tr, 1 dc, 1 h dc, 1 sc. There will be 6 groups in all
   4th rnd: 7 ch, 1 sc into the center st of the 1st loop, 5 ch, 1 dc between the 2 loops, 5 ch, 1 sc in the center st etc., all the way around
   5th rnd: work a curved shape, as in the 3rd rnd, into each of the ch st loops

Pattern 37: Flower rosette
Material: pearlized DMC yarn or other crochet cotton
Hook: 3
Work Plan: work in alternate rnds of chains and curved groups as in Pattern 36, increasing by adding to the chains or to the center stitches of each round
   Cast-on rnd: 8 ch, join in ring with ss
   2nd rnd: 3 ch (height of 1 dc) + 3 ch, 1 dc into 1st ch of cast-on rnd, 3 ch, 1 dc into next ch, and repeat around, into each of the 8 sts. Join ring with 1 ss into the 3rd ch of the beginning ch sts in the rnd
   3rd rnd: around each loop of ch sts work 1 sc, 1 h dc, 3 dc, 1 h dc, 1 sc. There are 8 groups in all
   4th rnd: 5 ch, 1 sc into the 1st dc of the 2nd rnd, repeat this for each dc
   5th rnd: around each loop of ch sts work 1 sc, 1 h dc, 5 dc, 1 h dc, 1 sc
   6th rnd: 7 ch, 1 sc in the space between the first 2 "petals," repeat all the way around, and join with 1 ss
   7th rnd: as the 5th, but with 7 dc as the center stitches of each petal
   8th rnd: as the 6th, but with 9 ch instead of 7
   9th rnd: as the 7th, but with 9 dc instead of 7 as the center sts of each petal

Pattern 37: Flower rosette. Rosettes such as these decorate the large rug shown in color plate 7 on page 4

Pattern 38: Classical rosette in a new form
Material: linen warp thread
Hook: 3
Work Plan: a simple pattern takes on new life because of the unusual material. The rosette is shown here is the bottom of a crocheted bag (see Pattern 39) but can be used on other articles or, decoratively, by itself

Cast-on rnd: 10 ch, join in ring with ss
2nd rnd: dc into space made by the ring
3rd rnd: 2 dc into each st
4th rnd: 1 dc, 1 ch, skip 1 st, repeat all around
5th rnd: 10 ch, join on where they started, 6 sc, 10 ch, etc. until there are 8 loops in all
6th rnd: 20 dc in each loop, working the first and last st of the group in the st that joined on the loop in the last rnd. When passing from 1 loop to the next, insert the hook in the preceding rnd with 1 sc
7th rnd: 1 ss in 1st 4 sts of loop, then 2 ch (which equals the height of the dc in this rnd) + 1 ch, skip 1 st, 1 dc, 1 ch, skip 1 st, etc., end with 4 ss in last 4 sts of loop. There are 6 dc on each loop. Continue with next loop in same way, but join the 2nd ch st into the last dc of the preceding loop, then 1 ch, skip 1 st, 1 dc, etc.

Pattern 38: Classical rosette in a new form

Pattern 39: Crochet bag with rosette base
Material: linen warp thread
Hook: 3
Work Plan: use the rosette in Pattern 38 as the base of the bag, and continue with the sides as directed below, in net crochet. The net consists of regular equilateral triangles of which the horizontal leg is 3 chain stitches, and each of the other legs is 1 triple crochet. An edging and draw-string are added after the sides have been worked to the desired height. The model is 12 triangles high

Pattern 39: Crochet bag with rosette base

Triangular net used in Pattern 39

Sides

1st rnd: Begin the 1st triangle by working 3 ch (which equal the height of 1 tr) + 3 ch. Bring yarn over hook 2 times, insert where the 1st 3 ch begin, and work tr but do not draw last loop through. Yarn over hook 2 times, skip 1 st, insert hook, and finish working tr so that there is only 1 loop left on the hook. In this way, you have joined the 2 tr that form the sides of the triangle. Begin 2nd triangle with 3 ch (see drawing) and repeat all around. Join rnd with ss to the center st of the 6 ch that began rnd

2nd and succeeding rnds: start with 6 ch, repeat as for 1st rnd

Edge

Work 1 rnd in dc

Draw-string

Make a crocheted cord, and thread it through the spaces of the triangles in the top rnd. If 2 cords are threaded through so that the bag is closed by drawing them in opposite directions, the bag will close more securely

Pattern 40: Rosette cushion

Material: linen warp thread; coarse linen thread
Hook: 3

Work Plan: use rosette like that in Pattern 38 as base for cushion. Note that in the model there are 7 doubles in each loop of the 7th round, rather than 6. Only 1 round of the triangular net (see Pattern 39) is used before the border, sides, and back are started. In the cushion in coarse linen thread shown in color on page 5 there are 8 doubles in each loop in the 7th round, and square net is used instead of triangular net

Border

1st rnd: 3 ch, sc in point of triangle, repeat along side. In each corner st work 1 tr, 3 ch, 1 tr, 3 ch, 1 tr, 3 ch, and 1 sc in point of next triangle. Continue next side as before

2nd rnd: 2 sc in each space on sides, 3 sc in spaces at corners

3rd and successive rnds: sc under both loops, 3 sc in each corner st. Continue this way until the cushion is the desired size

Pattern 40: Rosette cushion. A cushion based on the same pattern but with a square net is shown in color plate 9 on page 5

Sides and Back

Work in sc following the principles used in Pattern 23.

Cushion (color plate 9 on page 5)

The material is coarse linen thread, and the net crochet is in squares, not triangles, which is easier to work. You merely have to remember that the number of chain stitches must always correspond to the height of the stitches used to make the sides of the squares. If the chains are longer or shorter, a rectangular net will result

When the cushion has reached the desired size, reduce at the corners in one of the two different methods shown in the drawings. Then work in toward the center to produce a square opening through which you can stuff the pillow

Finish off by working all the way around the edge of the opening in double crochet, to give extra strength

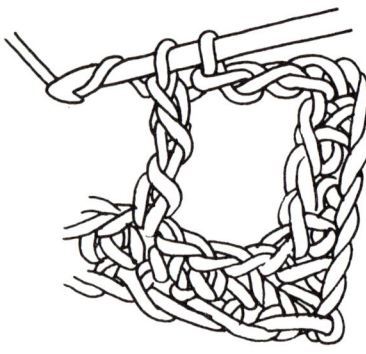

Reducing the net at the corners of the cushion in Pattern 40

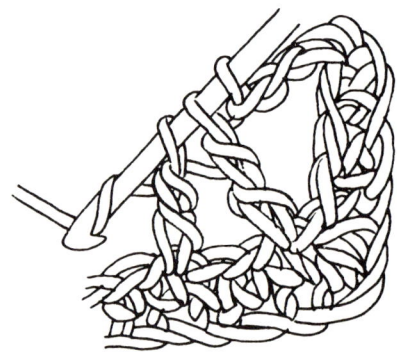

An alternate method for reducing the net at the corners of the cushion in Pattern 40

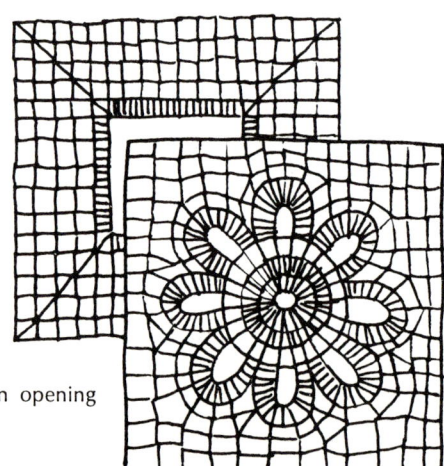

Front and back of cushion with square net, Pattern 40. An opening for stuffing in the cushion is left in the net at the back

FREE FORMS AND FREE USE OF COLOR

There is no limit to the number of variations that can be evolved by working rosettes or open star shapes quite freely, without any preconceived pattern. They can be worked in loose stitches so that the background shows through to advantage, or in thicker yarn with colors worked in without any particular system. The actual shades will depend on what you like or have available.

Free forms can be a purely artistic expression, like the wall hanging in Pattern 41. In such a work, one figure determines the next, and you need not be constrained by working into a regular outline or combining the shapes to form an even geometrical pattern, as long as the whole is visually pleasing.

Pattern 41: Wall hanging

Material: coarsely-twisted linen yarn. In the model, black yarn was used as this gives an almost graphic effect to the background net and to the irregular shapes of flowers and stars.
Hook: 3
Work Plan: the star shapes are the basis. They are worked first, and then embedded in the background, which can be made to resemble a spider's web or a fish net. The net, made chiefly of chain stitches, is sometimes closed, encircling the rosette figures, and sometimes open, merely holding them in their places. The result is like a fish net, full of the night's black catch of star fish and sea urchins

Pattern 41: Wall hanging

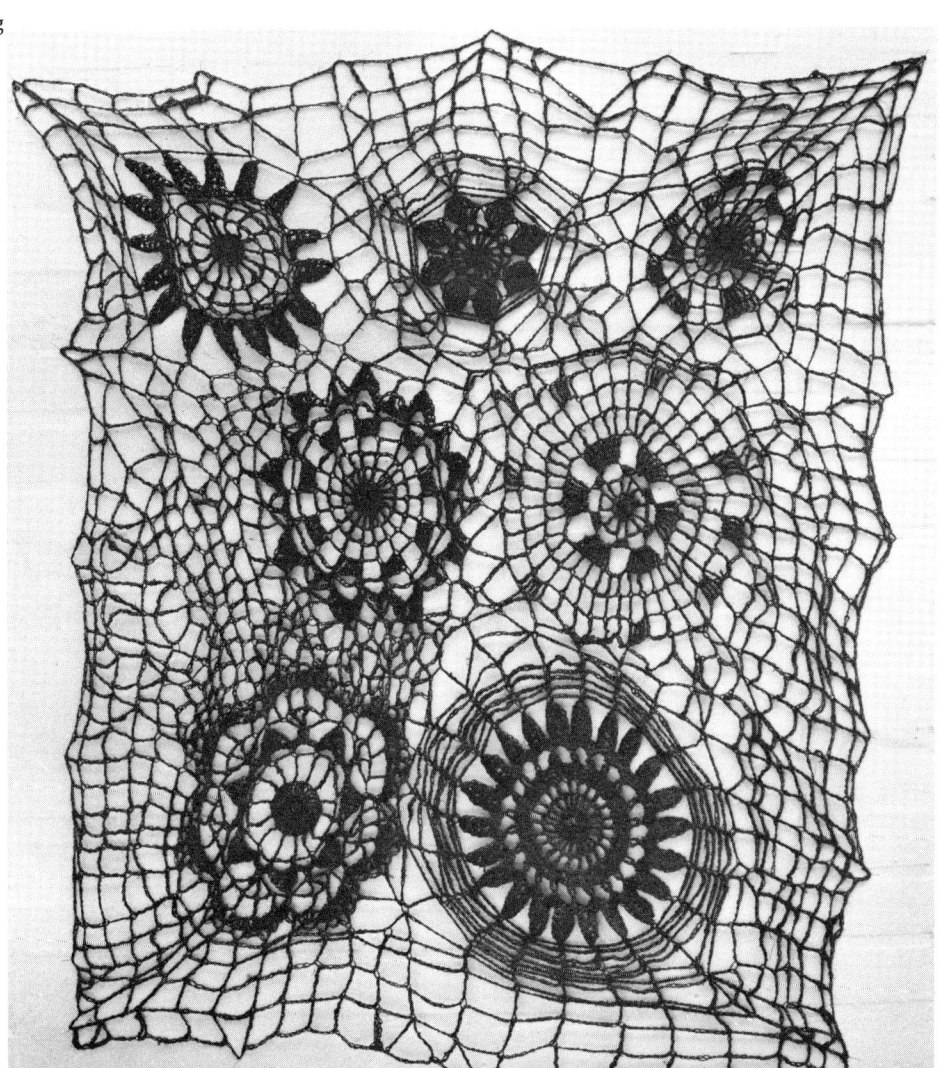

The net is made up of varying lengths of chain stitches, which are joined to the figures and to each other by the kinds of crochet stitches used in the stars and rosettes. The height of the stitches determines the kind of net that results

The drawing shows how a double crochet can be used to close a round in a ring shape, instead of using the slip stitch. You start with a set length of chain stitches—the drawing shows 5 chain stitches on each side except the last—and close with a section of fewer chains—in the drawing it is 3—and the multiple stitch you are using. The double crochet equals the height of 2 chain stitches, so that 3 chain stitches and 1 double crochet achieve the same length as the other sides (3 + 2 = 5). If you are using a triple crochet, you make only 2 chain stitches. By using this technique of closing rings you can further vary the effects in your free crochet

Pattern 41 allows for many variations. Here a ring is being closed with a double crochet

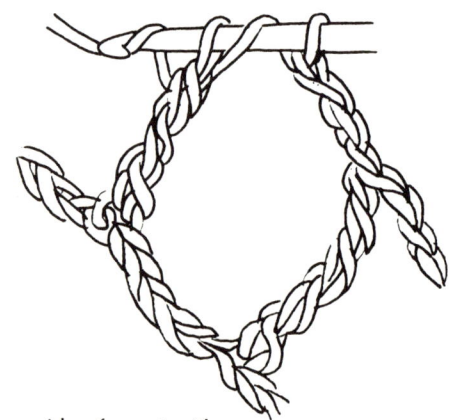

Another variation in free crochet is closing one side of a net with a multiple stitch. Here the double crochet takes the place of 2 chain stitches

Pattern 42: Winter sports helmet

Material: left-over pieces of thick sports wool, or rug wool, in different colors

Hook: 4½

Work Plan: a simple round hood with a slit for the eyes and nose is made by increasing from the crown downwards. The colors are worked in without any particular system, and for such frequent joining, a good method is to work a few stitches with double yarn, one strand of the old color and one strand of the new

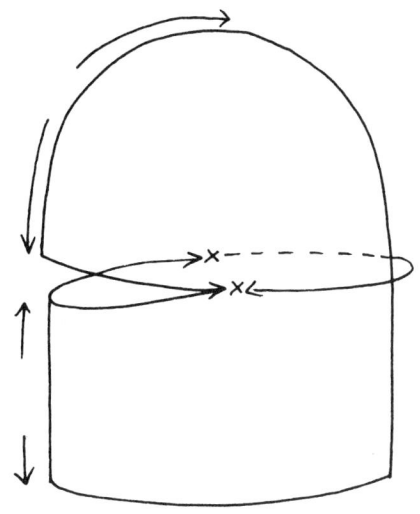

Helmet

Cast-on rnd: lay the yarn in a ring, work 8 sc over the ring, and close with a ss

2nd rnd: 2 sc in each st

3rd rnd: inc by making 2 sc in every other st

4th and succeeding rnds: inc in every 3rd st, 4th st, etc. until you have a crown about 8⅔ inches high and about 24 inches in circumference (22 × 62 cm)

Following rnd: work 34 ch st, starting at one side of the slit, and join into the previous rnd after leaving an opening of about 12 or 13 inches long (32 cm) continue with sc

Finishing rnds: sc without inc for about 4 more inches (10 cm)

Edging

Use the same edging color, in sc, on the bottom of the hood and around the slit opening

Slit in helmet in Pattern 42. After increasing from the crown down to the slit, crochet straight for about 4 inches (10 cm)

Pattern 42: Winter sports helmet, also shown in color plate 14 on page 6

STUFFED FIGURES IN CROCHET

Toys for children or other useful objects can be made from closed figures that are stuffed or padded. The hens in the photographs are descended from china hens (shown in the drawing) that were used in the old days to keep boiled eggs warm when they were served on the table. Here the same form is made from crochet, and is suitable as an egg or biscuit warmer. At the same time, the soft, light form is inviting for a small child (or the family cat) to play with, and nice for the child to lay his head on if he gets tired.

Stuffed figures in crochet can be very appealing. These are shown in color plate 8 on page 5.

Covered dishes made in the shape of hens were popular in northern Europe and England in Victorian times. Made of china or glass, these figurines were designed as egg cosies, to keep boiled eggs warm when served. Often they appeared on Easter tables. Today they are popular items in antique shops. (Drawing after *Victorian Glass*, Ruth W. Lee, Wellesley Hills, Mass: Lee Publications, 1944)

Pattern 43: A stuffed "china" hen in nest

Material: soft, natural wool, orange yarn, 2 glass beads
Hook: 8
Work Plan: the hen is worked from a bottom oval continuously up the sides, with the appropriate increases and decreases for the neck and head. It is then stuffed, and stitched closed down the back. The nest is worked in tunisian crochet, and folded in on itself to make a double layer for the hen to be set in

Pattern 43: A stuffed "china" hen in nest

The hen in Pattern 43 is started from an oval base

Hen

Cast-on row: 8 ch + 2 ch (height of dc)

2nd rnd: 3 dc into 8th ch, 1 dc into each of next 6 cast-on sts, 4 dc into last st. Now work on around to the other side of the cast-on chain, 1 dc into each of the cast-on sts, close with ss

3rd rnd: 2 ch, then 1 dc, then 2 dc into same st for next 3 sts, 6 dc, 4 × 2 dc, 6 dc, and close rnd with a ss

4th rnd: 2 ch, then 2 dc into each of next 6 st, which form the curve in front, 3 dc, 2 dc into next st (to give a little width at the sides) 4 dc, 6 × 2 dc (forms the curved back), 4 dc, 2 dc into next st, 2 dc, close with ss

5th rnd: 2 ch, dc all around except for the 2 center sts at the back, where you should work 1 dc + 1 tr into the 1st st and 1 tr + 1 dc into the 2nd st

6th and 7th rnds: dc all around

8th rnd, the head: 2 ch, 3 dc, dec by working 3 sts together in the center front, 4 dc, 1 h dc, 1 sc, then 3 ch, which are attached 2 sts before the 4 first dc, then 1 sc, 1 h dc, and close with 1 ss

9th rnd, the head: dc (there should be 16 in all)

10th and succeeding rnds, the head and beak: work 2 dc together all the way around, after which work the sts together in sc to finish the head. At this point work the beak: 2 ch (height of 1 dc), 2 dc inserted side by side at the root of the beak, cast off the dc together to form the point on the beak (see drawing)

Last round, the body: 4 × 3 dc together for the round at the back, and similarly dec in the 3 cast-on sts in the front at the neck

Stuffing and Finishing

Fill the hen with stuffing or other soft material, and stitch together down the back

Work each tail feather separately. Cast on 8-10 ch, and work back along the chain with 2 sc, 2 h dc, and the rest in dc. Then sew the tail feathers on

Finish the beak by binding it around and around with orange yarn, and work the comb in the same yarn in ch st—3 loops of 5 ch each. Attach to the head with sc

For the eyes, use 2 glass beads or stitch with yarn in a suitable color

Nest—bottom

Cast-on rnd: in double yarn, work 8 dc in ring, close with ss

2nd rnd: in double yarn, work 2 ch, 2 dc in each st all around, close with ss. The diameter should be about 4¾ inches (12 cm); add another rnd if the piece is too small

Nest—sides (tunisian crochet)

Cast on row: 16 ch

2nd row, forward: put the hook into the next to the last ch, bring yarn over hook, and draw it up into a loop that will be left on the hook. Repeat this with all the sts, leaving the last loop on the hook to be worked off on the return row

3rd row, return: bring the yarn over the hook, and draw it through the first loop. Then bring the yarn over the hook again, and draw it through the next 2 loops. Repeat this all along the row, until only 1 loop is left on the hook. This loop is the first loop in the next forward row

Succeeding forward and return rows: insert the hook from the front through the loop of the preceding row, bring the yarn over the hook, and draw it up as a new loop. Repeat this all along the forward row, and work the return row as in the 3rd row. Continue until the work measures about 24 inches long (60 cm)

Finishing Nest

Sew the short sides (the first and last row) together, to form the nest. Turn the sides over double, rib to rib, to form a double wall for the nest. Then sew this doubled piece firmly to the edge of the bottom. The nest is now ready for you to set the hen in.

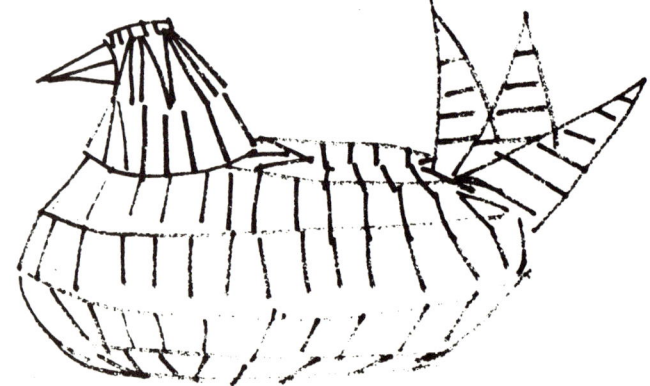

The body and the head of the hen in Pattern 43 are made continuously; the tail feathers are added later

COMPARISON OF SIZES OF CROCHET HOOKS AND NUMBERING SYSTEMS

mm.	steel (U.S.)	steel (U.K.)	aluminum or plastic (U.S.)	aluminum (U.K.)	wood (U.S.)	Giant plastic (U.S.)	New International numbering
.60		6½					.6
	14	etc.					
.75	13	5					.75
	12	4½					
1.00	11	4					1
	etc.	3½					
1.25	7	3					1.25
1.50	6	2½					1.50
1.75		2					1.75
		1½					
2.00	5	1		14			2
	4	1/0					
2.50	2	2/0		12			2.5
	etc.						
3.00	00	3/0	D or 3	11			3
3.50			E or 4	9			3.5
4.00			F or 5	8			4
4.50			G or 6	7			4.5
5.00			7	6			5
5.50			H or 8	5			5.5
6.00			I or 9	4	10 or I		6
7.00			J or 10	2			7
			K or 10½				
8.00					11 or L		
9.00					13 or M		
10.00							
11.00					15 or N		
12.00							
13.00					16		
14.00							
15.00							
16.00						Q	
17.00							
18.00							
19.00						S	

SOURCES OF SUPPLY

Macy's, New York, New York. Carries its own brand of many types of knitting worsted and other yarns, and sells imported and domestic yarns and cords of other manufacturers. Macy's brand 3-ply orlon fingering yarn is a good substitute for the thin two-ply wool called for in some of the patterns here.

Yarn Wholesalers. Write for a list of dealers if you cannot find these products in retail stores.

American Thread Co., 350 Veteran's Boulevard, Rutherford, N.J. Star Pearl Cotton is a 2-ply cord good as a substitute for the fish netting called for.

Coats & Clark, and J. P. Coats Co. 17-01 Pollitt Drive, Fairlawn, N.J. A supplier whose yarns may be found in stores in both U.S. and U.K. They make 2-, 3-, and 4-ply yarn, rug wool, mercerized and pearl crochet cottons.

Lily Mills Co., 395 Broadway, N.Y. Their Double-Quick 8-cord cable twist is a substitute for fish netting, and their Tru-Tone carpet warp could be used for the heavy linen yarn called for.

Pic Yarn Inc., P.O. Box 2010, Norwalk, Conn. 06852. A synthetic yarn with a different texture from wool, so loosely spun that it could be substituted for the thin natural wool. It is a 3-ply polypropylene yarn.

Reynolds Yarns, Inc. 220 Fifth Avenue, New York. Under its label it imports some very fine foreign yarns. Irish Knitting Wool is a 2-ply medium sized yarn, and Lopi is a natural mountain sheep wool from Iceland.

Bernhard Ulmann, Co. 230 Fifth Avenue, New York, N.Y. Special sweater and afghan wool, and Bear Brand thick 2-ply wool can be used where rug wool or thick rya wool is called for.